TEACHINGS TOWARD CHRISTIAN PERFECTION

introducing

THREE SPIRITUAL CLASSICS

Olive Wyon

Teachings toward CHRISTIAN PERFECTION

introducing

THREE SPIRITUAL CLASSICS

Christian Perfection by François Fénelon
Christian Perfection by John Wesley
The Spiritual Life by Evelyn Underhill

WOMAN'S DIVISION OF CHRISTIAN SERVICE
BOARD OF MISSIONS, THE METHODIST CHURCH

WOMAN'S DIVISION OF CHRISTIAN SERVICE
BOARD OF MISSIONS, THE METHODIST CHURCH
475 RIVERSIDE DRIVE
NEW YORK 27, N. Y.

Printed in the United States of America

LIBRARY OF CONGRESS CATALOG CARD
NO. 63-8291

CONTENTS

FOREWORD

THIS STUDY BOOK is an introduction to three spiritual classics. But it is more than that: it brings us into touch—through their lives and their writings—with three outstanding people whose whole lives were governed by one desire: the desire for God. This led them to a surrender and an obedience which is the heart of Christian perfection. Across the centuries these three are united in this one search and this one aim. Roman Catholic, Methodist, Anglican, all "are near enough to the Cross to touch the wood," and so "they are near enough to touch each other." Dr. W. E. Sangster is right when he says: "The saints of all communions are the saints of One Communion." Their lives are both an encouragement and a challenge. Dr. Sangster closes his great book on sanctity with these words: "The way is open for all. Holiness is not a monopoly of the cloisters, or of one branch of Christendom. The energies of the Holy Spirit are available to everyone who will seek Him."[1]

Recommended Materials

The *text, guide, classics,* and *supplementary materials* are available in special paperback editions from Literature Headquarters, Woman's Division of Christian Service, Board of Missions, The Methodist Church, 7820 Reading Road, Cincinnati 37, Ohio:

TEACHINGS TOWARD CHRISTIAN PERFECTION: INTRODUCING THREE SPIRITUAL CLASSICS by Olive Wyon. (text) $1

GUIDE by Dorothy McConnell. 50 cents

Classics:

CHRISTIAN PERFECTION by François de Salignac de La Mothe Fénelon, ed. & pref., Charles F. Whiston. $1.75

CHRISTIAN PERFECTION as believed and taught by John Wesley, ed. by Thomas S. Kepler. $1

THE SPIRITUAL LIFE by Evelyn Underhill. $1.25

Hardcover editions of the three spiritual classics are available from Cokesbury Book Store of your area.

Supplementary Materials

SELECTIONS FROM THE WRITINGS OF FRANÇOIS FÉNELON, arr. & ed. by Thomas S. Kepler. 15 cents

SELECTIONS FROM THE WRITINGS OF EVELYN UNDERHILL, arr. & ed. by Douglas V. Steere. 15 cents

SELECTIONS FROM THE LETTERS OF JOHN WESLEY, arr. & ed. by J. Manning Potts. 15 cents

JOHN WESLEY'S NOTES ON ROMANS. 50 cents

PRAYER CARD: *I am no longer my own, but* THINE (John Wesley's Covenant Prayer). 5 cents; 25 for $1

PRAYER CALENDAR OF THE METHODIST BOARD OF MISSIONS. Workers, work, and maps. 60 cents; 3 for $1.50

François Fénelon

and

CHRISTIAN PERFECTION

FRANÇOIS FÉNELON

NEAR THE HEART of France is a lovely region, sometimes called *The Land of the Three Rivers:* the Dordogne, the Lot, and the Tarn. These great green rivers swirl through limestone hills and wooded valleys. They are bordered by steep, rocky cliffs and often fringed with trees. On a hill near the Dordogne stands the ancient castle of the Fénelon family, with its medieval towers. It is surrounded by high walls and great trees. From the terrace in front of the castle there is a wide view over undulating country in which scattered rows of poplar trees give character to the landscape. Today this district is quiet, but when François de Salignac de La Mothe Fénelon was born, in the Chateau de Fénelon in Pêrigord, on the sixth day of August, 1651, the whole region was in the throes of civil war.*

Indeed, on Christmas Day, 1651, the siege of

* *Fénelon: L'Homme et L'Oeuvre* by Ely Carcassonne is the major source of the biographical data in this section. The quotations are translated by Miss Wyon.

Sarlat, a neighboring town, began. Suddenly the tocsin sounded, and very soon monasteries and convents were going up in flames. So when the little François was old enough to play about in the castle grounds with his brothers and sisters, or when he was indoors with his mother, he must have heard many a terrible story of towns being besieged and burned, of people suffering from famine and wounds and fear. We know that once his father had to arrange terms of surrender when a certain town could hold out no longer. Even after the fighting was over, the children were forbidden to wander far from the castle, not only because of danger from wolves and snakes, but because disbanded soldiers, hungry and desperate, were roaming the countryside looking for food and stealing it whenever they could. Often, too, they would attack passing travelers and hold them for ransom.

THE EARLY YEARS

In spite of the disturbances in the world around him, the boy François seems to have had a happy childhood. For inside the castle and its immediate grounds there was home and peace and love. François grew up with a great love of gardens and flowers and quiet beauty. How he must have loved the beauty of his own countryside! In springtime the meadows are still thick with flowers; the rocky cliffs by the river are often overhung with a wild creeper covered with blue blossoms, like a morning glory; and the nightingales sing night and day.

No stories of his early childhood have come down to us, but we know that he was his father's fourteenth child, the second son of his second wife. His family was very ancient; they had held these lands since the year A.D. 1000. Owing to various misfortunes in previous generations they were not rich, but they were aristocratic and distinguished. Fénelon's father died while the boy was still young, and his uncle, the Marquis Antoine de Fénelon, became his guardian. We know nothing about his early education but it must have been a good one—probably with a private tutor—for François was a very intelligent boy and learned his lessons very easily. The region in which he spent his childhood was full of a hidden but very deep religious life. Thus, while he was still quite young, he was being influenced by these religious movements. In the words of Ely Carcassonne: "Fénelon breathed this air."[1]

At the age of twelve François was sent to the Jesuit school in the ancient town of Cahors. This town is almost entirely circled by one of the Three Rivers, the Lot, which is spanned by a most beautiful bridge with three slender towers and six great arches. In the seventeenth century Cahors must have been an absolute jewel among all the towns of France, with its great twelfth-century cathedral. Though its exterior is grim, the north door of the cathedral is memorable: its subject is the Ascension, and the figure of Christ is deeply moving, the face expresses great majesty and profound tranquillity. Here the boy Fénelon must often have worshiped, though school prayers were said daily in a chapel close at hand, which still stands. The school itself is still there, close to the cathedral; and an open space nearby, with trees and grass, is named after Fénelon.

At this school Fénelon laid a good foundation for later studies in Latin and Greek. When he was fifteen—for some reason unknown to us—his uncle removed him from Cahors and sent him to the Collège du Plessis in Paris, which was attached to the University. Here Fénelon remained for several years, studying philosophy and theology as well as classical languages and other subjects. Apparently his progress was so rapid and he was so brilliant that his uncle became anxious about him. He was afraid the boy's head would be turned, and he gave him many a good scolding: "Can't you keep quiet? Don't talk so much! Try to imitate the silence of Jesus Christ!"

Fénelon's studies lasted for six years or perhaps for seven. When he left the University he already knew that he was called to the ministry. About 1672 his uncle sent him to the famous theological seminary of Saint-Sulpice in Paris where he came under the influence of a very wise and saintly man, M. Tronson, who became and remained Fénelon's friend and adviser through all his triumphs and trials.

THE AGE OF LOUIS XIV

If we are to understand Fénelon as a man and as a spiritual guide, we need to know something of the world which he entered when his formal education had been completed.

His whole lifetime is covered by the historic period known as the Age of Louis XIV [1643-1715], so designated because it was during this king's reign that a new kind of civilization arose in France, which, in its turn, had a great influence upon Europe as a whole. For one thing, there was a great improvement in behavior and in manners, and a remarkable development in the arts and in literature. Louis himself was called the "Sun King" by his admirers, and his court at Versailles, outside Paris, was the admiration of the whole of Europe. Even today the visitor to the town of Versailles is staggered by the traces of past magnificence. The Palace of Versailles—with its Hall of Mirrors, its aristocratic society, its wonderful gardens with their fountains, pools, avenues, and winding paths, with white statues gleaming through the trees—was a glorious place. But it was built upon a piece of wasteland, on a reclaimed swamp, by the forced labor of thousands of poor workmen.

Here, in the largest palace in the world, Louis XIV held his court. Lest his nobles should plot against him, Louis kept them all under his own eye. No one could stay away from court without being suspected of disloyalty to the King, and absence was highly dangerous for the person concerned. Since the King's power was absolute, few dared to incur his displeasure, for he could ruin a man with a word. Outwardly, all was splendor; the courtiers passed their time in servile admiration of the King, in trivial amusements, in intrigues and scandals, and in the enjoyment of every luxury that that age could provide. Everything the King did—not excluding his less moral and, to put it mildly, less dignified actions—was loudly applauded. His obvious faults were either glossed over or ignored.

France meanwhile was in a sorry state. Crime was rampant, even at the very gates of Paris. In many parts of the country the burden of royal taxation was so heavy that there were frequent revolts, which were always crushed with cruelty and brutality. But most of the courtiers at Versailles knew little about these things and cared less. To do him justice, Louis did try to improve the administration, and, when he heard that people were rioting for bread, he had a good deal of bread given away to those who asked for it. But this did not touch the root of the trouble. As the King's love of power increased, he grew away from his subjects; only his glory mattered to him. So the beauty of Versailles was in no way representative of the state of France during the Age of Louis XIV.

One of the great men of this period was the wise and merciful military engineer, M. Vauban. He traveled all over the country and saw the France of that day as it really was. As the King's friend he knew the splendors of Versailles, but he also saw the other side—the miseries of the country folk, the soldiers whose wages were not paid till they were desperate (indeed Vauban often paid them out of his own pocket). He visited the prisons and found out how unjust the laws were; he saw the terrible results of religious persecution and pleaded for the men and women of the Reformed faith who were being forced into exile. He saw the roads full of homeless beggars. And as he traveled he counted—

that is, he collected statistics. He found that one-tenth of the entire population of France were beggars; five-tenths, almost beggars; three-tenths, poor and in debt. What about the remaining tenth? These were the rich and the fortunate. Why were there so many poor? He looked into this carefully and discovered various causes for all this misery: the constant wars; the profligate extravagance; but most of all the scandalous system by which the rich, who already owned land and wealth and other possessions, paid no taxes. This meant that the whole expense of the King's pleasure, including his buildings, his wars, and the government of the country, was being borne by the poorest people. Later on, toward the end of Louis XIV's reign, the state of the country was so bad that—in spite of his absolute power—criticism of the monarchy began to assert itself.

Fénelon, who had been at court, was well aware of the serious situation. In an anonymous letter which he wrote to the King—possibly about 1695—he pointed out that the Dutch War should never have been undertaken; he poured scorn on the King's military preparation and then attacked Louis himself: "You are praised to the skies for having impoverished France, and you have built your throne on the ruins of all classes in the state. France is a great almshouse destitute of provisions."* Whether this letter ever actually reached the King no one knows; historians take different views; but, in any case, it did reach someone and was a bitter indictment of all that the "Sun King" stood for. Though no one could then foresee the future, it is not too much to say that the seeds of the French Revolution of 1789 were sown during this long reign.

After 1685 the King's health declined; many of the great men of his time had now died, and he was left alone, "the last survivor of an age which all these illustrious men had honoured, and he went down to his grave sad, defeated, a burden to himself and to others, leaving France without industry, without commerce, exhausted, and cursing even that great reign which for twenty-five years she had hailed with enthusiastic applause."[2] What Victor Duruy said of the sixteenth century could also be said of seventeenth-century France, using Voltaire's now famous phrase: "It was a bloody robe of silk and gold."[3]

* This letter goes on: "You have spent your whole life ignoring the way of truth and justice, and consequently, ignoring the way of the Christian gospel. . . . You do not love God. You do not even fear Him except with a slavish fear; it is Hell, not God, that you fear!" (Quoted by Ely Carcassonne in *Fénelon: L'Homme et L'Oeuvre,* p. 88.)

IN PARIS AND AT THE COURT

Now we must go back to the story of Fénelon. We left him at the Theological Seminary in Paris. An excellent student, he read and studied widely and deeply. Above all, under the wise guidance of M. Tronson, he learned a great deal about the deeper side of the spiritual life, for this was what he wanted most. At the end of his three-year course he was ordained and was at once appointed to serve as a curate—assistant—in the parish surrounding the great Church of Saint-Sulpice. He was young, brilliant, full of ideals and good desires. At one time he even dreamed of going on a mission to some distant land—which would have been a very great adventure in the seventeenth century! But he was already a disciplined man, and he accepted willingly the regular round of parochial duties.

The parish was poor, dirty, noisy, and often rebellious. It swarmed with children. Fénelon taught them their catechism and, we may guess, held them spellbound with his stories. He loved children and had a great gift for storytelling. Now and again he preached and expounded the Scriptures. From what we know of him, he must have been an eloquent preacher. This was a happy time for Fénelon: he was witty and humorous; indeed, in spite of many troubles, to the end of his life he remained young in heart. Here, too, at the very outset of his ministry, he began the great work of his life: that of a pastor and guide of individual souls. Old and young, rich and poor, experienced Christian believers and people who wanted to believe: they all came to him, young as he was. In the words of a modern French writer, "To illuminate, comfort, and direct souls occupied him from his youth up, and was to occupy him all the days of his life."[4]

In 1678, when Fénelon was already becoming well known, he was offered the post of head of a society for women recently converted to the Roman Catholic Church; it also took in young women who wished further religious instruction. In those days all Protestants were "heretics," and in many instances they were harried and persecuted unmercifully. But Fénelon carried out his mission in a gentle and generous spirit. He was, of course, true to the rigorous principles of the age in which he lived, but the spirit in which he carried out his mission and later preached to the Calvinists of Saintonge comes out very plainly in the following prayer which he wrote at this time:[5]

O GOOD SHEPHERD, *Grant that we may henceforth become one flock, one heart and soul. . . . May all Thy children work together for a real reformation, in peace and in humility, trusting in Thy mercy, in order that Thy Church may regain her youth, and be radiant with the beauty of her early years.*

During these years (1678-1688) Fénelon's sphere of influence had been growing. He had many friends at court and was already greatly admired and loved by an inner circle of dukes and duchesses who were trying to lead a Christian life in the midst of the worldly distractions of the court. At this time Louis himself admired and trusted him. So it did not cause great surprise when, in 1689, on the sixteenth of August, it was announced that Fénelon had been appointed tutor to the Duke of Burgundy, the King's grandson, who was in the direct succession to the throne of France. This was both a great honor and a great responsibility. This new position placed Fénelon at the very heart of a society where he knew he could serve great ends. He would now have access to the King himself, to his wife, Madame de Maintenon, and to the various ministers of the Crown. Above all, the education of a future king of France was in his hands.

Fénelon's pupil, the young Duke of Burgundy, was not an easy boy to educate. When Fénelon took him over, he was seven years old. Already he had been badly spoiled, and was so arrogant that he thought he was a very special being, and looked down on everyone else. He would have been the despair of most teachers, for he was already very greedy, self-indulgent, and—if he was thwarted in any way—would give way to almost insane fits of passion. At the same time, he was intelligent, open, and truthful. He was the kind of boy who would be described today as "temperamental"; fortunately, Fénelon preferred such boys to the more placid type. As his tutor, Fénelon was not merely expected to teach him his lessons, but also to train him in character and to try to prepare him for his future vocation as king of France. Fénelon's methods were very wise: he did not preach at the boy, nor did he scold him more than was absolutely necessary. He tried to reduce the violence of his temperament by gently leading him to accept a moderate discipline in ordinary life: in food and drink, in physical exercise, as well as in other ways. Fénelon's aim was to teach and train him through living experience rather than by formal or moral exhortations. For instance, if the young duke had been exceptionally arrogant, or had given way to anger and had been making scenes, he was not whipped, nor was he put on a diet of bread and water. He was simply—and quietly—made to feel that people around him were displeased or disappointed. This was the general principle on which Fénelon based his training: instead of regarding the boy as an *exceptional* being, whose every whim ought to be indulged, he was training him to realize that although, or because, he expected one day to be king, he *needed* other people, he needed to have personal relations with all kinds of people.

As a teacher, Fénelon excelled. Grave and serious as he could be, he knew how to enter into the mind of a child. At first he taught him a great deal through stories, many of which were of his own invention. With his lively gift for storytelling, the charm and nobility of his personal character, and his real affection for his pupil, it was no wonder that very soon the boy fell under his spell and looked up to him with love and reverence. To anticipate a little: Fénelon worked a miracle upon this difficult boy. To the amazement of the court, the young Duke of Burgundy grew into a prince who was gentle and courteous, modest and kindly. He married young, and very happily. But in 1712 he and his young wife died within a few days of one another.

So Fénelon's pupil never became king of France. But in 1689 all this was hidden in the future.

For several years Fénelon exercised a great influence at Versailles. He was at the height of his powers and his reputation when a cloud appeared in his sky. It was to grow larger and darker as time went on, until it burst into a storm which changed the whole current of his life.

THE QUIETIST CONTROVERSY

Suddenly, Fénelon's popularity began to decline. There were whispers going round, suspicious looks, a certain coldness on the part of people who had hitherto been friendly. Then came a time when Fénelon was sharply criticized, when his former admirers—especially among the clergy—argued with him and shook their heads over him. What had happened? All this difficulty arose, quite unwittingly on his part, out of his perfectly natural and healthy friendship with a woman named Madame Guyon. He had met her for the first time in the year 1688. He was then thirty-seven and she was a widow of forty. Madame Guyon had been a widow for twelve years, and through sorrows and difficulties she had grown into a rich spiritual life; this led her to write one or two small books which had a great influence among educated people, especially at the court, where she was welcomed and valued by Madame de Maintenon herself.* It was through these friendships within the sophisticated court circle that she came to meet Fénelon at the house of a mutual friend. At once she felt that Fénelon needed some spiritual help, and she knew she could give it. He, on his side, realized that here was someone who could "speak to his condition." For years, in spite of all the good that he was doing, he had been feeling perplexed and dissatisfied. After their first meeting he corresponded with Madame Guyon. He also found much help in her writings. How was it that she—an untrained woman—was able to help this brilliant and devoted man?

Evelyn Underhill suggests that Madame Guyon had a very deep religious experience and that this accounted for the affinity between Madame Guyon and Fénelon. Apart from this there was never any other element in their relationship to one another: in fact they met seldom. Unfortunately, however, Madame Guyon lacked the intellectual gifts she needed to express her thoughts. She expressed herself badly, used words loosely without realizing that they would be misunderstood. She wrote a great deal: her autobiography covers more than 700 pages; it is an ex-

* Madame de Maintenon was the second wife of King Louis XIV. Since she was not royal she never became "queen," but she had a great influence over the King and, through him, on public matters.

traordinary document, containing simple narrative and much religious common sense as well as many extravagant statements. For a time she was very popular in the religious circles at Versailles. Then suddenly the storm broke. At first it only seemed to be a tempest in a teapot. Indeed, even today some French writers, who have studied the whole story closely, think that Madame de Maintenon suddenly became jealous of Madame Guyon's influence over Fénelon, resented it, and started the unfortunate ball rolling. Whether this was the case or not we cannot tell, but it may have been one element in a difficult situation.

The situation became serious when the word "heresy" was mentioned; for in those days, and under Louis XIV, to be suspected of heresy was a terrible, shocking, and dangerous thing! So when bishops and theologians came thundering down upon poor innocent Madame Guyon, it was because they suspected her of heresy—the heresy of Quietism. Fénelon became involved because it was known that he had some sympathy with her teaching. He was, of course, aware that she was often unwise in her manner of expression, both in conversation and in writing. But he had received a great deal of help from her at a critical time in his life, and although he did not agree with many of her statements from the point of view of theology, he was far too honest and chivalrous to abandon her now when she was at the mercy of keen ecclesiastics eager to denounce her as a heretic. He did his best to defend her—with disastrous results for himself. At court he and Madame Guyon were suddenly dropped like a stone. Then Madame Guyon was imprisoned, and Fénelon—who was already Archbishop of Cambrai when the storm broke—was banished from Paris. Later on, the King forbade him ever to leave his diocese.

What was this so-called heresy, Quietism? It sounds innocent enough! Its chief representative was a man called Molinos (1640-1697). It was his teaching which had just been condemned at Rome. Much of his teaching was true and valuable, but he went too far, and his followers went farther still. What had happened was this: at that time there were many people in Europe who could not find a living faith in the formal religion of the day. These people felt a great need for a simpler and more personal contact with God. In England, this need was met by the Quakers; sometimes—at the beginning—some of them also went too far; but they soon righted themselves and settled down as a religious community with a deep life of its own, which has made, and still makes, a great contribution to the church and to the world. Molinos had tried to meet this need by his insistence on "the freedom of the spirit . . . simplicity towards God . . . surrender . . . silence":[6] all perfectly good and true. But unfortunately some of his followers exaggerated this "freedom": many of them threw over all the outward, necessary practices of religion, such as attendance at public worship, Bible reading, "saying prayers," self-discipline. In some cases they even discarded all the principles of ordinary decency and morality. They claimed to be "free" because they were following an "inner light." Any sensible person can see where they went wrong: they were divorcing their religion from life as God had given it and as he meant it to be lived; they were trying to live as though they were "spirits," instead of sinful, ordinary human beings, needing the grace of God and his help at every moment of their lives.

It seems almost incredible that this error should have persisted in different forms, though not under this name, even down into modern times. For instance, as late as 1933, eight members of a family of Kentucky mountaineers were arrested and imprisoned on a murder charge. They had together conspired to murder Lucinda Mills, aged 72; the prisoners included two sons of Mrs. Mills, two daughters, two sons-in-law, her daughter-in-law, and her grandson. When they were questioned, some of them told the police that "they had received a divine command to make a human sacrifice and that the lot fell upon Mrs. Mills. A son-in-law is alleged to have said that he wanted to prevent the sacrifice, but he had a feeling that he must not."[7] This is the "inner light" carried to a wild extreme, justifying the caustic remark that sometimes "the inner light leads to the outer darkness."

When we take such possibilities into account and when we realize how easily a scare or a witch-hunt may arise even in modern times, we need not be surprised at the excitement over Madame Guyon and her teaching among people who did not understand what she was saying. Added to that, there was so much gossip and superstition associated in the popular mind with any kind of new doctrine that the outbreak of this storm is something we can readily understand. A modern example would be a communist scare in a town or country which is violently anticommunist, especially if it affects people in high places. At the first hint of danger, suspicion and fear give rise to all sorts of rumors, and often a quite innocent person may be caught in a trap, and even punished for something that happened long ago or for something which he was supposed to have said. Very often such a person is merely a scapegoat.

In this instance, Madame Guyon, a good, innocent,

The Cathedral of Cambrai
Cambrai, France

things up in the air, and that some kind of decision about her teaching ought to be made. He contented himself at first with removing Madame Guyon from St. Cyr.

The next step was the setting up of a semiprivate inquiry; this was in the hands of three people only: Bossuet himself—as Bishop of Meaux; De Noailles—Bishop of Chalons; and the wise and able M. Tronson—the President of the Theological Seminary of Saint-Sulpice. These meetings went on for nine months, from July, 1694, to March, 1695. Before the close of these conferences Fénelon became the fourth member of the board, for he had just been nominated to the Archbishopric of Cambrai. His influence counted for a great deal in the final stages of the Issy Conferences: in the end Madame Guyon was not condemned, and Fénelon still supported many of her views.

But further troubles were brewing. Both Bossuet and Madame de Maintenon were disappointed and angry at this inconclusive result—as they regarded it. The enemies of Fénelon were watching and waiting to see which way things would go. Indeed, Madame de Maintenon now seemed to have made up her mind either to save Fénelon or to break him! ("If only he would give up defending Madame Guyon!") Bossuet, too, seemed now to have come to the conclusion that Madame Guyon's teaching was a danger to the Church and ought to be stamped out. For a short time the fire smoldered. Then it flared up into the famous controversy between Bossuet and Fénelon, sometimes described as the "Battle of the Giants." This aroused passionate interest and concern, and rival groups were formed for or against. But the details of this historic struggle need not detain us here. It is evident that a great deal of harm was caused by the talk and intrigue which went on behind the scenes, both inside and outside the court and the Church. All kinds of false rumors and slanders were set in motion and were repeated everywhere. Bossuet himself descended to personal accusations and to behavior that would now be considered out-of-place even in a newspaper of the least reputable type. He betrayed confidences, and even published a private letter of Fénelon to Madame Guyon—of course out of its context—in order to try to give a false impression. Madame Guyon meanwhile was still in prison, being harried by police interrogations, having been arrested in December, 1695. She stuck firmly to her guns, for she had nothing to hide.

Fénelon had already taken up his work at Cambrai and was coping with the difficulties of new work and a new diocese under great strain.

Since this "battle" was fought out mainly on paper, the two books written by the two protagonists brought things to a head. In February, 1696, Fénelon drew up his "Notebooks of Issy" and revised, rewrote, and published them in the autumn of that year under the title, *Explanation of the Maxims of the Saints Concerning the Inner Life.* He hoped that this calm objective statement about what the saints down the ages had always believed and experienced would clear up the matter. He had taken great trouble over this book and had gone through it with theologians, who had pronounced it "correct and useful." When Bossuet saw this book actually in print, he was almost beside himself with rage; he hurried on with his own book which appeared a month later under the title, *Instructions on the States of Prayer.* Much of it was ill-informed and open to criticism, but it appealed to a great many people, and it stirred up still more bad feeling against Madame Guyon and Fénelon.

In desperation Fénelon appealed to Rome. After a long process of inquiry and discussion the Pope—who did not want to condemn Fénelon—condemned his book, but in very mild terms.[8] Fénelon accepted the verdict with dignity and without bitterness. Louis XIV banished him from the court, dismissed him from his position as tutor to the young prince, and ordered him never to leave his diocese. Madame Guyon was kept in prison till 1703. Fénelon's enemies rejoiced, his friends were loyal and cast down. But Fénelon accepted his public "disgrace"—as it was in the eyes of a great many people—quietly, and threw himself heart and soul into his new work at Cambrai. "Disgrace" seems hardly the word to use of such a man.

FÉNELON AT CAMBRAI

Fénelon had been nominated Archbishop of Cambrai on the fourth of February, 1695. A few months later he went to Cambrai and began his work. At this time he was still in favor with the King, and it looked as though Madame de Maintenon hoped that a distant diocese would separate him from Madame Guyon, and that all this "nonsense" would stop. To some of his friends this appointment gave no pleasure. But the post he had been given presented no easy task. Cambrai had only been ceded to France eighteen years before (by Spain) and to rule such a diocese well and wisely would be a very difficult and delicate matter. Fénelon had certainly not expected such promotion and was not in the least elated by it. For whether he was rich or poor, honored or criticized and slandered, he always remained himself. At the height of the Quietist controversy, in 1697, his palace at Cambrai was burnt down. He lost nearly all his books and papers. Yet he never complained. During those first difficult years in his diocese, he kept his feelings to himself, was faithful in duty and free from bitterness. He lived what he taught, accepting the will of God in every situation. He "remained at Cambrai what he had been all his life: an apostolic man, whose zeal took many forms."[9]

This vast diocese in the north of France, some of it extending over the border into the Low Countries, was not an easy one to administer. As Cambrai had only belonged to France for a few years, most of the inhabitants were not pleased to be under French rule. The country was thickly populated. Convents and monasteries abounded, and some of them were rather unruly and disorderly and needed a firm hand over them.

When Fénelon first reached Cambrai he felt very lonely. Wherever he went he felt that the people looked upon him as a "foreigner"; and they bitterly resented foreign rule. Worse than that, they all knew that he had come straight from Versailles, from the court, and the people of this diocese certainly did *not* appreciate His Majesty Louis XIV. Added to all this was the heavy responsibility of the task which awaited him: a diocese with 764 parishes, scattered over a vast area.

From his own letters from Cambrai at this time we can see how wisely he approached the people of his new diocese, how shrewd and astute he was in delicate situations, and also how down-to-earth in his understanding of life. He knew when to take things lightly and when to take them seriously. He set himself to know and understand local customs, and he treated them with respect. After a time, the general suspicion and hostility faded away. People knew that he was keen on justice and, when necessary, would stand up for their rights.

For instance, a story is told concerning a pompous official who ordered the inhabitants of Solesmes to repair their roads in *midwinter*. The people involved were desperate; so a deputation went to see the Archbishop: he listened to them and said, "I'll see to it." He wrote at once to the official who had given the order saying that these poor people would be hopelessly ruined, and all their carts and wagons would be destroyed, if they had to do this work in the midst of winter. He suggested that it would be more useful to the royal service if the men could wait to repair the roads in the spring, as the work was not urgent. Of course the official postponed the work, and the whole town was relieved. So the people knew that in their Archbishop they had a very human friend: when his carriage appeared in a village they all ran out to meet him, not to gape and to stare, but to talk to him, to tell him their troubles, and to ask his advice. He was indeed a good shepherd.

Fénelon traveled constantly all over his diocese, often leaving the main roads and bumping over muddy farm tracks and bridle paths to reach remote villages and hamlets. In one such spot he found there was no chapel within miles, so he had a little church built. He also visited the monasteries regularly, where he often found some irregularities and a low level of spiritual life. Sometimes he had to deal with unruly monks and he gave them "severe lessons in obedience." He was distressed to find in some houses that old and infirm monks were being unkindly treated by their fellows; then he would plead for them with all the gentleness and charm that he could use. Thus in every way he tried to reform his diocese. Now and again the peace of the countryside was broken by wars which flared up on the frontier. Fénelon did all he possibly could to relieve the sufferings of the soldiers and the inhabitants, not only with money, but by personal service, hospitality, and help of all kinds.

There is one delightful story which has come down to us from the Eulogy for Fénelon by d'Alembert before the French Academy. A number of peasants were lodged in his palace as they had been driven from their homes. Seeing one young man looking very sad and troubled, Fénelon asked him what it was about. He told the Archbishop that, when he had to leave the village, his enemies had made off with his cow. "I'll buy you another cow," said the Archbishop. But the young man would not be comforted; he wanted his *own* cow! So Fénelon called a manservant to him and together in the darkness they set out on foot to the village which was not very far away. Toward midnight the Archbishop returned—with the cow!

One endearing trait in his character, as we have seen, was his love of children. The large and dignified palace was cheered by the presence of several small boys, great-nephews and others whose parents treasured the influence of their friend on the young boys before they had to go on to more advanced schools. Several of the young clergy lived there as chaplains and secretaries, and some of them taught the boys regular lessons, but they all had their meals with their "Uncle." Doubtless when he had time he would charm them with stories of adventure and heroism and would draw their young hearts to the love of God.

What did Fénelon look like? About the time he was appointed to Cambrai this is what one very shrewd courtier saw: a tall, thin man, well-built, very pale, with a great nose, and eyes which flashed with fire and intelligence. It was a very curious face, so grave and so courteous and yet so gay and pleasant that this observer said he could hardly take his eyes off it.

Just because he was so busy and had such a heavy responsibility, from time to time he would withdraw himself for a few days to think and pray. One of his favorite retreats was the Cistercian Abbey at Voucelles which stood in a solitary valley between two rivers. Here there was a large thirteenth-century church and a beautiful garden. There he would walk up and down the shady paths, examining his own heart and conscience:[10]

> *I am myself a great diocese, more overwhelming than the outward one; and I don't know how to reform it. God opens a strange book for us when He makes us read what is at the bottom of our hearts.*

It was out of these retirements that he emerged to preach and to teach, to guide and inspire, comfort and encourage the people among whom he lived.

One of the greatest signs of the reality of his faith and prayer was his hard-won humility. This comes out very plainly in a letter written two days before his death. Evidently he did not know his correspondent, a lady who had expressed a strong desire to see him in order to tell him something "for his good." She had not approached him personally, but through other people, none of whom was known to the Archbishop. In spite of this round about method of appealing to him, he wrote to her with great courtesy, explaining that owing to his "peculiar circumstances" (i.e., his virtual exile) he could not visit her, but that he would be very ready to listen to her if she would write to him direct and tell him what she had on her mind and heart. He wrote:[11]

> *Although I have a position of pastoral authority, so far as I personally am concerned I want to be the last and the least of the children of God. I am ready—I believe—to receive advice and even correction, from all souls of goodwill. . . . So, if you have something to say to me which you think God has given to you, speak freely to me, without constraint. . . .*

In spite of rather frail health, Fénelon remained active and fresh in mind and heart to the end of his life. All his aloofness had disappeared. A recent writer says he seemed to have entered a new *spring-time!* He took the rough with the smooth, tried to renounce himself in everything, was full of charity, both in his heart and in actual practice. All he had was at the disposal of others. Although his benefice was a rich one, he lived frugally and, when he died, left neither debts nor money. His grace and charm were remarkable; even people who were prejudiced against him at a distance were fascinated when they saw him.

During the autumn of 1714 his health had been rather poor. Unfortunately, just after Christmas, on a dark winter night, as he was on his way back from a pastoral visitation, he had a serious accident. His carriage was crossing a bridge when suddenly a cow appeared on the roadway, startling the horses, who took fright and ran away; the carriage was overturned and wrecked. Fénelon was extricated from the debris and carried back to the palace. At first there did not seem to be much the matter beyond bruises and shock. But, soon after writing the letter to the unknown lady, he became very ill. He died on January 6, 1715. His last words were the prayer which sums up the spirit of his life:[12]

Thy will, not mine, be done.

FRANÇOIS FÉNELON'S CHRISTIAN PERFECTION

BEFORE WE BEGIN to study Fénelon's writings on *Christian Perfection*,* there are still one or two other points to be considered. The letters in this book have been chosen from a mass of correspondence filling several volumes. This collection is a sample of the kind of thing that Fénelon wrote during the whole course of his life without any thought of publication. This means, inevitably, a certain amount of repetition. But this is good, for it means that we can see for ourselves the main points of his teaching.

Further, they are letters of *spiritual direction*. That is, they are letters written to people whom he had been guiding and helping, often for a long time. These people looked to him and spoke to him frankly about their difficulties, their doubts, and their temp-

* All quotations in this section from *Christian Perfection* by François Fénelon are from the 1947 edition, edited and prefaced by Charles F. Whiston and translated by Mildred Whitney Stillman. They are identified only by the number of the page on which they appear and are used by permission of Harper & Row, Publishers, Inc., New York.

tations. As we read this book, we shall notice, here and there, that a letter is headed: "To a Person at Court." (See pages 7, 13, 16, 19, 57, *Christian Perfection.*) When we remember what it meant to live, day in, day out, at the court of Versailles, we begin to realize that its atmosphere—for Christian people—must have been stifling. The fact that this court life had a veneer of religion only made it worse.

Yet, even in this unhealthy atmosphere, there were people of another kind: dukes and duchesses and other nobles whose duty compelled them to live at court, but who were sincere Christians and were trying to lead a pure and good life in the midst of this strange mixture of great courtesy and beauty and vile and gross behavior.

So none of these letters were written to people living a quiet life. They were to persons in the heart of the world; and *there* they had to lead a Christian life, carrying out the duties of their calling, even when it meant wasting hours and days and weeks which they would far rather have spent away in the country, living quietly with their families in their own homes.

To such people Fénelon was the greatest comfort and strength. For, in addition to his many other gifts and graces, he excelled in this ministry to individual people. As we have seen, this work began while he was still quite young, and he continued it until practically the day of his death. *He understood the human heart so well because he understood his own.* His letters are so simple, so searching, and so direct, that his words come to us over the centuries with the force of something said *now—to us.* He himself was a rather complex person; that is why he could understand simple people. He was an aristocrat and could thus understand courtiers. Indeed, he understood these worldly people very well: he knew how fastidious they were, how often arrogant and impatient, how often they were disappointed in themselves when they began to see their faults in clearer light.

Fénelon's letters are something quite unique in religious literature. They breathe a charm which even today calms and delights us. Some of this power to soothe—and yet to inspire—came to him from the influence of Madame Guyon. He helped *her*, it is true, but *she* also helped him—a great deal.

As we read these letters we see how closely he followed his "spiritual children" in thought and prayer: not only in the early morning when they could be alone and pray, but in the office, or the study, or the drawing room, or among the chattering courtiers, when their buzz of conversation filled the galleries of the palace at Versailles. There, too, he tells them, "You can pray."

. . . word seeds
in the ground
of the mind and spirit . . .

THOUGHTS
ON READING SPIRITUAL CLASSICS

Before we begin to read and study this book or any of the classics, it would be wise to read Dr. Whiston's "Introduction" to Fénelon's *Christian Perfection.* Notice especially what he says about reading *slowly* (p. xi). If we are eager and interested we tend to fly at a book and gallop through it—at least if we are quick readers! There may be some books where this is all that is needed in order to get a general idea of the subject. But here we are reading in quite a different way: we are reading to *learn* something, and this kind of reading does not depend upon an *effort* to remember, but upon the *spirit* in which we *read.* A great spiritual writer used to say that this kind of reading might be compared to putting a lozenge in the mouth and just letting it dissolve. Nor do we chew it up in argumentative discussion but simply gently absorb what has meaning for us.

Then, as Dr. Whiston reminds us, we are reading the words—the actual words (if you were in France now you could see the actual letters, handwriting and all) of a very great man—"a truly great saint of God." They are *living words* because they spring out of costly experience. [What François Fénelon, John Wesley, and Evelyn Underhill have recommended each has tested and practiced.]

Dr. Whiston also urges us to relate this kind of reading to prayer. Such reading is indeed another form of meditation. We begin by praying that God will speak to us through these words. We read quietly and very slowly, and suddenly a word or a thought *hits* us. That is a sign that we should stop at once, think over this word, and then turn it into a prayer which springs from our heart and is related to our own life. "A very little at a time" should be our general rule. Many of us may find that we need to read these letters over and over again; each time we shall find more in them. When we do this it might sometimes be a good idea to write down the actual words which have helped us in a small notebook and then look up some passages of Scripture which bear on these points. In that way we shall be indeed feeding on the Word of God coming to us through the words of Fénelon.

Now let us turn to the book itself, rereading carefully Dr. Whiston's "Introduction" on *how* to make devotional reading most effective (pp. ix-xiii).

. . . the love
which God has for us . . .
gives us everything . . .

. . . the greatest gift
that He can give us . . .

FÉNELON'S MESSAGE

A modern French writer, François Varillon, says of Fénelon: "Like everyone who has a deep experience, Fénelon always had one thing to say—and one only." This "one thing," which he said both to theologians who opposed him and to courtiers and men and women of the world who sought his help, was his doctrine of *Pure Love:*[13]

> *It is the love which God has for us which gives us everything; but the greatest gift that He can give us is to give us the love which we ought to have for Him.*

This message is so simple and so profound that it meets and satisfies the human heart in any situation, on any level, and in all circumstances. It simply means loving God for himself and giving oneself to him with all one's heart. When we think about it, we can see that this is really the heart of the gospel: "Thou shalt love the Lord thy God with all thy heart. . . ."

But some people thought Fénelon's teaching was too difficult to be believed: "It's impossible for human beings to love like that," they said. But Fénelon simply went on saying it, to the very end. And how right he was. On the purely human level we ourselves know the difference between the mother who sacrifices herself for her children and thinks nothing of it, sends them out into the world to serve God and the community without any thought of herself. And we know the other kind, the mother who fusses over her children and tries to guard them from every kind of outside influence till they are almost smothered! Such a mother makes it very difficult for a son or daughter to go out into the world and fulfill the purpose for which they have been made. Yet this kind of mother says, "I love my children so much, I can't do without them! And, after all, look at what *I* have done for them and given up for them! Surely it's time they did something for *me!*"

"Pure love" is something very lovely, very simple, and not nearly so rare as complicated people think it is. God loves us purely and simply, and he wants us to love him like that, too, and everyone else as well. As a modern English writer puts it: "Lust and sentimentality separate, but love unites." This author, Gerald Vann, describes a family "that is living in love" as "one of those lovely homes where the doors seem always to be open and the rooms always full—full of all sorts of oddities as well as of all sorts of loveliness, full of the waifs and strays of society, as well as the immediate circle of friends,"[14] because it is full of love. But although Fénelon's message was one and the same always, he could express it in a hundred different ways, with an infinite delicacy of sympathetic understanding. His one aim was to reach the heart of each person to whom he wrote; for that, he knew, he needed a spiritual grace which would reach each heart in God's time—and in God's way.

He was very patient and would wait sometimes for years before he could say something searching to a person in need. He realized that there is a right time for everything, and that we must not rush ahead and try to do people good in our own impetuous, ignorant way. Often, he said, we have to wait until we know that the moment has come when our friend can receive the word of God through us. When Fénelon knew people well, and when he believed that the moment *had* come, he did not hesitate to be very direct. I wonder how the duchess to whom the following letter is addressed really *liked* it! "I must confess, my dear Duchess, that I am delighted to see you overwhelmed with the sight of your faults and your inability to overcome them!"[15] He goes on to explain what he means: that to *see* our faults is really a gift from God, because it opens the way for a "closer walk with God."

. . . pure love is . . .
singleness of will . . .

. . . *what men lack most,*
is the knowledge of God . . .

KNOWLEDGE AND EXPERIENCE

As we read and reflect upon these letters, I think most of us will feel that—on the human side—they have a great appeal. One of the reasons for this must surely be that Fénelon was a very honest man. Although he does not often speak about himself, we know by instinct that he is writing to his friends out of an experience which was often very like their own, and that *he understood their difficulties because he had gone through similar ones* and was perhaps even now struggling with them. Not only in this collection, but in many other parts of this vast correspondence, he gives a hint now and again of his own reactions to difficult periods and circumstances. Evidently he was well acquainted with what Carl Jung calls the "shadow side of God," and thus with the "darkness" in his own heart, for he often speaks in his letters of the presence of the cross, of inner dryness, and of the danger of becoming discouraged.

Here are some of the expressions he uses which throw a flood of light on the advice he gives to others:

> *The cross is everywhere; I can taste nothing save bitterness.*

> *I know by experience what it is to feel one's heart withered, and disgusted with all that must bring comfort.*

> *I am experiencing a shameful weariness of the cross.*

When he wrote of "the surly solitude of pride" or of the "cross of inner dryness," he was confessing his own knowledge of these psychological quicksands, which so often ensnare people who have no one to guide them through and bring them safely out on to firm ground.

It is precisely *because* Fénelon, himself, had such a painful experience of self-knowledge that he was able to help so many people. For, strange as it may first seem, this honest acceptance of his actual state —often in the midst of very trying outward events—

was the source of some of the most profound counsel he was later able to give to others. To one friend he wrote: "I am in a state of very bitter peace." What did he mean? How can "peace" be bitter? The answer to this question comes in another letter:

> *But what, you will ask, are you to say in seasons of dryness, coldness, and weariness? Still say what rises in your heart. Tell God that you cannot feel His love, that you are empty and cold, that He wearies you.*

In other words: we must learn to hand ourselves over to God, just as we are, keeping nothing back, for God understands us and will help us during these cold seasons of difficulty.

Scattered throughout the present book we can find further traces of this teaching (p. 53):

> *We are tempted to believe that we are no longer praying to God, when we stop finding joy in prayer.*

> *To undeceive ourselves, we must realize that perfect prayer and love of God are the same thing. . . . It is a love which loves without feeling, . . . as pure faith believes without seeing.*

. . . in the depth of the abyss
. . . we begin to find a foothold . . .

DISSIPATION AND SADNESS

In another passage he speaks about dissipation and sadness (pp. 93-101). By "dissipation" he does not mean indulgence in worldly pleasures but rather those wandering thoughts which often plague us when we are most desirous of praying to God. This distracted state of mind may be due to several causes: physical (overfatigue or ill health), or to some pressing anxiety or trouble. On the other hand, these distractions may be quite involuntary; then they are simply tiresome and are best ignored. By "sadness" Fénelon means what we usually call depression or discouragement. These moods, which come to us all at some time or another, are also due to different causes, and we need to learn how to distinguish between them.

All that Fénelon says on this subject is full of wisdom. Here is one passage (p. 95):

> *Often sadness comes because, seeking God, we do not feel his presence enough to satisfy ourselves. To want to feel it is not to want to possess it, but it is to want to assure ourselves, for love of ourselves, that we do possess it, in order to console ourselves. Nature beaten and discouraged is impatient at guiding itself in a state of pure faith. It makes all its efforts to get out of it because there all support is lacking. It is as though up in the air.*

Then he points out that a good deal of this sadness or depression is simply due to injured pride: we would like to see ourselves perfect, and we are disgusted at the sight of our faults! The only way out of this quandary, as Fénelon says, is to hand ourselves over, as we are, to God, keeping nothing back, for (p. 96),

> *When we are thus ready for everything, it is in the depth of the abyss that we begin to find foothold. We are as serene about the past as about the future. We suppose all the worst that we can of ourselves, but we fling ourselves blindly into the arms of*

> *God. We forget ourselves, we lose ourselves; and this forgetting of self is the most perfect penitence, because all conversion only consists of renouncing self to be engrossed in God.*

Closely connected with what Fénelon has to say about dealing with our moods of depression and discouragement is the stress he lays upon *the dangers of a religion based mainly on feeling*. This point is important for us today, for often quite unconsciously we tend to equate religious experience with certain emotions or delights. This is evidently no new temptation, for Fénelon has a good deal to say about it. At the time he wrote I imagine he was thinking of people he had met and perhaps tried to help, who were excited about Quietism or Mysticism and who were apt to think that religion consisted in having extraordinary experiences, visions, and the like. Fénelon admits, of course, that such experiences may come to any of us when God sees they will help us at a certain stage in our lives; the danger comes when we hanker after such things, when we may even try to "work them up." Like babies, we, too, have to be weaned and learn to eat the strong meat that God provides (pp. 151-152). Above all, we need to take our eyes off ourselves and try simply to obey God in daily life and in the willing acceptance of discipline and suffering when it cannot be avoided.

Overemphasis upon visions and feelings can indeed be a great danger (p. 152):

> *He who has no other support will leave prayer, and with prayer God himself, when this source of joy is exhausted.*

St. Teresa, he reminds us, said that "a great number of souls stopped praying when prayer began to be real" (p. 152).

The second point he makes is that people who seek for "realization" in order to find "assurance" only end up in disappointment or in illusion: for they are placing their trust in their feelings and their imagination instead of in God (p. 153):

> *It is only pure faith*
> *which saves from illusion.*

This subject recurs in his letters again and again. His teaching is sound and true, and is in line with all that the great saints like St. John of the Cross and others have taught down the ages.

. . . we must refer everything to God, or to ourselves. . . .

SUFFERING AND SELF-RENUNCIATION

Then he goes deeper still, and tackles the questions of suffering (p. 170) and self-renunciation (p. 178). Here, as in all his writings of this kind, we notice that Fénelon is a shrewd psychologist! He may have lived in the seventeenth century—but his advice is based on sound insight into the workings of the human mind. For instance, in a recent book on *Guilt* which deals with all kinds of psychological difficulties, the writer points out that every attempt to get rid of a sense of sin uses one or all of these three mechanisms of escape; i.e., people try to evade *self-knowledge*, *suffering*, and *responsibility*.[16] We have seen how Fénelon deals with self-knowledge; now we see why he lays so much stress on the value of suffering. He does not speak of it as a *problem* (as we tend to do), but as a *fact* to be recognized, faced, and accepted (p. 88):

We know that we must suffer, and that we deserve it. However, we are always surprised at the suffering as though we believed that we neither deserved it nor needed it. It is only a true and pure love which loves to suffer. . . . A will satisfied by that of God, when all else is taken away from it, is the purest of all loves.

In a later passage Fénelon explains the value of spiritual suffering—of those shattering experiences of desolation which some people (and often the best) have to go through. This kind of suffering, he says, is needed in order to purify us from the residue of sin, which is largely unconscious; we only perceive it when we are in the grip of inward suffering. God is like a surgeon who has to inflict pain in order to heal (pp. 170-171):

It is our corrupt self-love which makes our pains. The hand of God hurts as little as it can. . . . We find God by himself, only in this apparent loss of all his gifts, and in this real sacrifice of our whole self, after having lost every resource within.

But though we may feel "like a tree withered to the root," he advises (p. 173),

> *. . . wait until the winter is past, and until God has made all die which ought to die, then the spring revives all.*

So when we are passing through such an experience we can say with faith, "If Winter comes, can Spring be far behind?"

There is a close connection between this acceptance of suffering of all kinds and *the practice of self-renunciation.* On this subject Fénelon's counsel is both wise and shrewd—as well as very searching. Those to whom he wrote must have sometimes shivered as they felt that he could see right through them! How surely he traces the workings of our self-love in all its windings and in all its disguises! Look at this disguised self-love—evidently drawn from life: "We see a person who seemed to be all for others and not at all for himself, . . . a person who seems self-disciplined, self-forgetting." Yet it is easy to unmask this kind of "modest pride" which is "impatient of criticism. If the people whom it loves and helps do not repay it in friendship, respect and confidence, it is hurt to the quick. . . . It does not need dull praises, nor money, nor success. . . . It does, however, want to be repaid. It is hungry for the esteem of good people. It wants to love so that it will be loved, and so that others will be impressed by its unselfishness. It only seems to forget itself in order to make itself more interesting to everyone" (p. 179). Of course this is not all thought out and logical, but at bottom this is what this kind of "goodness" is worth. If even good people can be so self-deceived, how can most of us get away from ourselves? (p. 180)

> *It is only the love of God which can make us get out of ourselves. There is no middle way. We must refer everything to God, or to ourselves.*

But if that were all the advice Fénelon has to give us, it might seem as though such liberation would be wholly impossible. He then balances his stern uncompromising statements with the other side. He shows how gently God leads us along the path of self-renunciation, only asking of us what we can give at a certain moment (pp. 191-192):

> *There is a veil of mercy behind which God hides from us what we should not be able to bear.*

. . . a humble waiting under the hand of God, and a quiet bearing ourselves in this state of darkness and dependence, are infinitely more useful to help us die to ourselves than all our restless efforts to advance to our own perfection.

Let God act, and let us be content to be faithful to the light of the present moment. It carries with it all that we need to prepare us for the light of the moment to follow.

. . . there is no middle way . . .
we must refer everything to God . . .

. . . you can do the will of God . . .

HOLY WORLDLINESS

Holy Worldliness is another concern with which Fénelon deals. The expression may sound new, but Fénelon's letters show that the idea was not new even in seventeenth-century France. It is worth noting that out of the twenty-eight letters in Part I of this collection no less than seven are specifically addressed to persons "living in the world" or at court. Fénelon suggests, or rather seems to take for granted, that the ideal of Christian perfection can be realized upon earth even in the midst of conditions which seem most alien to it. When we read these letters we should constantly remind ourselves of the kind of life these nobles were forced to lead in the artificial atmosphere of the court at Versailles under Louis XIV. Here are the words of a French historian who, speaking of the absolute domination by the King, says: "This general condition of slavery showed itself most of all in the court, where Louis kept the nobles in gilded captivity. Versailles had been built with this design; all France was kept there under the eye and hand of the King. . . . Three conditions had to be fulfilled to win the favour of the King: to demand and secure a lodging at Versailles, to follow the court everywhere, even when ill or dying, and to approve of everything."[17] In the later years of this reign scandals increased to such an extent that one of the most famous courtiers wrote that the court "sweated hypocrisy" under a king turned pietist. For those without strong character, and without a living faith, the result was appalling. Vice in the highest circles flaunted itself. The terrible results were felt most of all in the following reign; and before the close of the eighteenth century came the explosion of the French Revolution.

In the light of these facts read the letter addressed to a person at court (p. 13): "Golden chains are no less chains than are chains of iron. . . . Your captivity is in no way preferable to that of a person held unjustly in prison. . . . You have nothing more than he except a phantom of glory." The whole of this letter is written with inside knowledge of the conditions under which this person was living, and yet even there, says Fénelon, "You can do the will of God" and thus be pleasing to him.

. . . *moment by moment*
enter into God's plans . . .

RIGHT USE OF TIME

The use of time (p. 3) and the question of recreation (p. 7), referred to in the first letters, should be understood in relation to the strange artificial life which these people were forced to lead. Fénelon checks any tendency to have unreal and exalted ideas about Christian perfection by his teaching on the absolute importance of fidelity to the will of God in the smallest and most ordinary details of daily life. Here again he is certainly down-to-earth. He urges his courtly correspondents to realize that it is not so much *what* we do as the *spirit in which we do it* that matters: in that way we can serve God truly wherever we are.

. . . *you have nothing more*
than he . . .

. . . to whom we owe all . . .

GOD THE CENTER

Finally—and most important of all—in reading these letters and extracts from Fénelon we should take special note of the point of view from which he writes: *for him everything begins and ends in* God. He is "theocentric," as the theologians say. We in the twentieth century tend to be man-centered and self-centered. Fénelon reminds us that (p. 113)

> *what should stir the truly faithful is the idea of a God who is all, who does all, and to whom we owe all.*

It is because we do not know God that we do not love him, says Fénelon (p. 116). So he ends as he began, by speaking of the doctrine of pure love: The love of God for man and our response in self-forgetting, adoring surrender in love to God and to man.

John Wesley

and

CHRISTIAN PERFECTION

JOHN WESLEY

ONE BRIGHT AFTERNOON in May, 1742, two travelers rode into Newcastle through the old city gate. They looked around them with pleasure: "What a fine place!" they exclaimed, as they rode past the castle and along the pleasant streets full of old and beautiful houses which stood back from the road in spacious gardens and orchards. It was springtime and all the fruit trees were in bloom; the air was full of the scent of lilac, and here and there the gold of laburnum mingled with the beauty of apple blossom. The two travelers found an inn, stabled their horses, and set out to explore the town. Soon they came to some narrow streets which led down to the river. The further they went, the more depressing were the sights that met them: the houses were poor, often dilapidated, and very dirty; the nearer they came to the river, the more closely were the buildings huddled together.

It was a lovely evening; men, women, and children were standing about or strolling along; the children, who looked dirty and neglected, were playing and quarreling; the men were often cursing and swearing, and many were rolling about dead drunk. "What misery!" said the older man to his companion, "surely this is the place for us!"

Next morning (which was Sunday) at seven o'clock the stranger—a neat, spare man with piercing eyes—walked with his younger friend to the end of a wretched street in the older part of the town. There the two men stood still and began to sing:

> MAKE a joyful noise unto the LORD,
> all ye lands.
> Serve the LORD with gladness:
> come before his presence with singing.

And so on, through the Hundredth Psalm. Three or four people ran out of their houses to see where the sound was coming from. Then others joined them; the excitement grew, and in a short time there was a crowd of some four to five hundred people. Then the leader began to speak on the words, "He was wounded for our transgressions . . . and by his stripes we are healed." No sooner had he begun to speak than a deep silence fell upon the crowd. Meanwhile more and more people came up until nearly fifteen hundred stood there listening as, with infinite tenderness and freedom, he spoke to them of the love of God—for *them*. When the preacher stopped, the people still stood there, gaping and staring, in astonishment. The speaker saw that they were amazed, so he said quietly and courteously, "If you desire to know who I am, my name is John Wesley. At five in the evening, with God's help, I design to preach here again."

In the evening Wesley chose a hill nearby for his open-air pulpit. By five o'clock the whole hill was packed with people from top to bottom. The people hung upon his words as he pressed home the message:

"I will love them freely."

When Wesley finished there was a great silence; then, as he turned to go, people pressed upon him so that he could hardly move. As he reported in his *Journal*: "The poor people were ready to tread me under foot, out of pure love and kindness." At last he managed to reach his inn, where several persons were waiting for him: "Stay with us at least for a few days," they implored him, "or at least for one more day!"[1]

During an amazing ministry of fifty years such scenes occurred again and again.

THE EARLY YEARS

John Wesley was born on the seventeenth of June, 1703, during the later years of Fénelon at Cambrai, some twelve years before his death. No one could have guessed that the little boy born that summer day into a rectory in a remote part of England was going to be as famous as the great French Archbishop. John's father was the rector of Epworth in Lincolnshire from 1697 to 1735—thirty-nine years of unrewarded, difficult, heartbreaking work. For several years his parishioners, a wild lot, treated him and his family with hostility, sometimes even with violence. So it was in no quiet backwater that the Wesley children grew up.

John was the fifteenth child out of nineteen. The income of the rector was quite insufficient for his family's needs, and Mr. Wesley was almost always struggling with money troubles; once he was even imprisoned for debt. But in spite of everything, the Wesley children had a happy family life bound together by love, order, and discipline. Their mother Susanna was, as we all know, a most remarkable woman. She trained her children in self-control, obedience, courtesy, and diligence. She was their teacher as well as their mother; their formal education began when they reached the age of five. Then they had regular hours of work as strictly observed as though they were at school.

The story of the rectory fire is famous, but it is worth repeating because it had so much influence on Wesley's later life. The fire broke out on February 9, 1709, between eleven o'clock and midnight. Through some oversight little John was in great danger but was rescued in the nick of time. In about fifteen minutes the whole house—together with the furniture, clothing, books, and papers—was completely destroyed. But the rector showed his spirit when he called out to the men who had saved John: "Come, neighbours! let us kneel down; let us give thanks to God! He has given me all my children . . . I am rich enough!"[2]

All through his life Wesley never forgot this experience. One important result of John's escape from death was the effect it had upon his mother. Two years later she wrote in her diary of private meditation: "I do intend to be more particularly careful of the soul of this child, that Thou hast so mercifully provided for, than ever I have been; that I may do my endeavour to instil in his mind the principles of Thy true religion and virtue. Lord, give me grace to do it sincerely and prudently, and bless my attempts with good success."[3]

When John was about twelve he left home for

school, and in 1720 he went to Oxford to study. He passed through his years as a schoolboy and an undergraduate with ease and grace; he did not give up the outward observances of religion, though other things mattered much more and his religion was rather formal. But he was never touched by the demoralizing influences of Oxford life at that period. At the beginning of 1725, however, after five years at Oxford, he began to feel a great desire for more reality in religion and for a deeper spiritual life. He read and thought and prayed. Gradually the idea of becoming a clergyman began to take a strong hold on his mind.

He consulted his parents, and their replies were so wise and so illuminating that he went forward with his preparation with a very earnest resolve to give his life to God as fully as possible. On September 22, 1728, he was ordained a priest in the Church of England, ready to serve his church in any way she might appoint. For a time—apart from a period spent in the country helping his father with parish work—he found his vocation in university work at Oxford where he had been appointed a Fellow of Lincoln College in 1726. It was during these last six years in Oxford that "Oxford Methodism" came into being. It started as the "Holy Club," a little group consisting of the Wesley brothers and a few others, who took their religion so seriously that they were an object of mockery and laughter to many of their contemporaries. Later George Whitefield joined them.

On April 25, 1735, John's father died. A few months later all the members of the "Methodist" group had to go out into the world to their various callings. John and Charles Wesley had been asked to go over to Georgia to help with mission work among the Indians as well as with the new colonists. The story of their experiences is well known. In spite of working with great devotion, John was not happy there; he was often tactless and unwise and managed to get involved in some unpleasant tangles which were only cut by his leaving for home at the end of 1737. During his long winter voyage he tasted the bitterness of disillusionment. Like Fénelon before he met Madame Guyon, Wesley was approaching the turning point in his life. But he did not understand himself and, during those early weeks of 1738, he went through much painful heart-searching. He began to doubt whether he had ever been a Christian at all. Later he wrote, referring to this period of doubt and uncertainty:[4]

I had even then the faith of a SERVANT, *though not that of a* SON.

He himself felt that he was useless and defeated, and his soul was in darkness. Others, however, judged differently. When Whitefield went out to Georgia a few months later he said: "The good Mr. John Wesley has done in America is inexpressible . . . Oh! that I may follow him as he has followed Christ."[5]

THE CRISIS

The crisis which was to mean everything to John Wesley, and everything to thousands of people in his lifetime and beyond, was now approaching. Wesley was being prepared for something greater than he knew. Just as Fénelon met Madame Guyon at a similar moment, so Wesley met Peter Böhler, a young Moravian minister, who was a great help to him. Böhler insisted that he was to continue preaching whatever he felt, and faith would come.[6] Wesley obeyed, but his heart was heavy and he was often in great distress of mind. On Wednesday, May 24, 1738, John woke at five o'clock; at once he opened his Bible at the words, "There are given unto us exceeding great and precious promises." In the afternoon someone called and asked him to go to the service in St. Paul's Cathedral. The anthem for the day was: "Out of the deep have I called unto thee, O Lord. . . . O Israel, trust in the Lord; for with the

LORD there is mercy, and with him is plenteous redemption. And he shall redeem Israel from all his sins" (Ps. 130:1, 7-8, *Book of Common Prayer*). That evening, most unwillingly, he went to a religious meeting to which he had been invited in Aldersgate Street, in the city of London. During the meeting, one of the persons present read aloud from Luther's *Preface to the Epistle to the Romans*. The next morning Wesley related in his *Journal*:[7] "About a quarter before nine, while he was describing the change which God works in the heart through faith in Christ, I felt my heart strangely warmed. I felt I did trust in Christ, Christ alone, for salvation; and an assurance was given me that he had taken away *my* sins, even *mine*, and saved *me* from the law of sin and death."

For him "revelation" had become personal.

This personal experience of Wesley's was epoch-making in more senses than one.* For the moment, however, we are thinking simply of John Wesley as a man—a man in great distress—who has at last found peace. Evidently some of his distress had been caused by secret struggles against resentment, for which he doubtless felt he had every justification. He had been thirsting for God—yet he had been

* William E. H. Lecky—the historian of the eighteenth century—said that the hour of Wesley's conversion was "an epoch in English history."

inwardly unreconciled, at least in thought, with certain persons, possibly in the recent past. Now, when he knew that he was forgiven, at once his whole outlook was changed: "I began to pray with all my might for those who had, in a more especial manner, despitefully used me, and persecuted me." Forgiveness made him forgiving.

Even then it was not all plain sailing, he still had to fight against doubts and temptations. "Where is your joy?" was one, and he then reflected that the "feeling" of joy is given or withheld by God, and that what he had to do was to hold on in simple faith: "I was much buffeted with temptations, but cried out and they fled away." The entry in his *Journal* the next morning reads: "The moment I awaked, 'Jesus, Master,' was in my heart and in my mouth; and I found all my strength lay in keeping my eye fixed upon him, and my soul waiting on him continually."[8]

Like St. Paul, he now felt that he must go away for a time and find strength and refreshment in another setting. So he went to Germany for three months, where time to think and pray and a great deal of contact with good German friends, including a visit to the Moravians at Herrnhut, helped him to get settled in his new life.

In September, 1738, John returned to England. At once he began preaching to small groups in various halls and churches. But it was in April, 1739, that the call came which sent him out to his lifework. It all happened very naturally, and almost incidentally.

In his *Journal* for March, 1739, he says: "During my stay [in London] I was fully employed between our own society in Fetter Lane and many others, where I was continually desired to expound; so that I had no thought of leaving London, when I received . . . a letter from Mr. Whitefield . . . entreating me in the most pressing manner to come to Bristol without delay."[9] John was not at all anxious to leave London, where—it seemed to him—he had found a sphere of service which would probably expand as time went on. But at last he saw that he ought to go to Bristol. There he found that Whitefield had just begun the "strange way of preaching in the fields." Wesley was almost shocked by it, "having been all my life (till very lately) so tenacious of every point relating to decency and order, that I should have thought the saving of souls almost a sin, if it had not been done in a church."[10] On April 2, convinced by Whitefield's arguments, he consented to preach in the open air. It had cost him a great deal to come to this decision. We can see how he felt about it when we read what he says in his *Journal*: "At four in the afternoon, I submitted to be more vile, and proclaimed in the highways the glad tidings of salvation, speaking from a little eminence in a ground adjoining to the city, to about three thousand people."[11]

THE WORLD TO WHICH WESLEY CAME

When Wesley stood up to preach in the open air on that April afternoon in 1739, he had stepped out into a different world. Behind him lay a world of scholarship and civilized living. John seemed to be cut out for quiet work among thoughtful and well-mannered people. Suddenly, without much choice—as it seemed to him—he had been thrust out into a work which he would never have chosen and one which was to absorb all his energies. What was this new world into which he had entered? What was it like? Church life at this time was often at a very low ebb. In the words of Bishop Butler, too often Christianity had become "a subject of ridicule" because it "interrupted the pleasures of the world."[12]

There was a great gulf between the prosperous, elegant, complacent upper and middle classes and the people at the other end of the social scale: they were often in extreme want and misery, especially in the towns. An English Methodist says of those days: "The treatment meted out to the common people by the rulers of eighteenth-century England is one of the saddest and most tragic chapters in our social history."[13] There were appalling social evils. Before 1759 there was the "gin era," which sent up the death rate at an alarming pace. There was the terrible waste of infant life; travelers could not bear to see bodies of babies littering the edges of the roads as they went toward the capital while the ordinary people "passed by on the other side." There was the dreadful state of the prisons, which is often mentioned by the Wesley brothers who visited them as much as they could. This scandal was intensified by the panic legislation passed by Parliament to increase the number of crimes which were punishable by death. English Law at this time has been described as "a sanguinary chaos." Men and women, boys and girls lay in Newgate and other prisons under sentence of death for "crimes" like stealing a sheep or a handkerchief. John and Charles Wesley made a point of visiting condemned prisoners and doing all they could to help them. Charles speaks of spending the last night in a cell with several men whom he had led into peace; they sang their favorite hymn * at intervals during the night and at the last moment before their execution the next morning.

* Behold the Saviour of mankind
Nailed to the shameful tree!
How vast the love that Him inclined
To bleed and die for thee!—Samuel Wesley (1661-1735)

Once John Wesley had stepped out into this strange new work of preaching in the open air, he knew he had found his vocation. He never looked back. Henceforth he was free to go wherever he was sent to declare the message which God had given him. Whether indoors or out, to thousands or to two or three in a wayside inn, it did not matter. To them all he proclaimed the free, overwhelming love and mercy of God.

As we read Wesley's *Journal*, one of the first things that strikes us is the fact of the enormous crowds which flocked to hear him. The scene at Newcastle, with which we began, though in itself a very important one, is only a sample of the effect of his preaching. The *Journal* abounds in laconic expressions like the following: "I went with Mr. Whitefield to Blackheath where were, I believe, twelve or fourteen thousand people. . . . I preached . . . in Upper Moorfields, to (I believe) six or seven thousand people. . . . At five I preached on Kennington Common, to about fifteen thousand people on those words, 'Look unto me and be ye saved, all ye ends of the earth.' . . . I declared to about ten thousand, in Moorfields, what they must do to be saved. My mother went with us, about five, to Kennington, where were supposed to be twenty thousand people."[14]

Naturally we ask ourselves: Why did people flock to hear Wesley in these vast numbers? and that not only at the beginning of his ministry in the open air, when it was a novelty, but to the end of his long life? It must have been that the moment he began to speak every one of his hearers felt, "this means *me*": it was a "word" from God himself. This was *God's* moment—a day of his visitation—and he was using his messenger, John Wesley.

Even though these masses of people often listened to Wesley with deep attention, now and again—and especially during the earlier part of his ministry—the listening silence would be broken by loud cries and catcalls as rough men rushed into the crowds and very soon created a seething mob. Usually these attacks came from outsiders, who were often incited or encouraged by people who ought to have known better. The violence of the mob was a well-known feature of the eighteenth century: Wesley often spoke of it as "the beast," and it certainly was both ugly and appalling. Such violence may have been unconsciously due to the sense of frustration of people who were often in the last extremity of misery and were therefore against anyone better off. But it was not always due to these causes; sometimes it was quite senseless. Wesley met these attacks with great courage and calmness. He found that, if he could single out the ringleader when the trouble began, he could usually stop him by sheer personal courage and courtesy. He would go straight up to the man looking him straight in the eyes, and in a few moments, no one knew quite how or why, the storm would die down. But there were other times when this was not possible, and John and his brother and other Methodist leaders were in danger of their lives.

The most impressive thing about this apostolic ministry of nearly fifty years is its quality and its power, which is scarcely hinted at in the *Journal*. To preach several times a day, to travel all over the "three kingdoms" (England, Scotland, and Wales) mostly on horseback, over dreadful roads sometimes no more than rutted tracks or swampy trails over wild moorlands, in dangers from highwaymen, in dangers from storm and flood, wind and snow, was in itself a physical achievement. But to go on doing this year after year, day in, day out, offering the gospel message with the same urgency, compassion, and living reality, almost to his last breath, was nothing less than a miracle. No wonder that sometimes, when he was old and famous, people would go in thousands to see him passing through a town, to "gape and stare, as if the King were going by."[15]

WESLEY'S SOCIAL CONCERN

John Wesley was not only the Apostle of England, not only a great preacher who could use very forceful and even violent language on occasion, he could also be a "very angel of gentleness; and men and women all over the three kingdoms loved him for it."[16] The very texts from which he spoke showed how tender and compassionate he could be; and this brought God very near. But though he was used to speaking to people in their thousands, he never thought of them in "masses"; to him they were all persons—each one precious in the sight of God. But over and over again in his writings (and they were many) he showed that he had no use for excessive individualism; he insisted that Christianity is "essentially a social religion, to turn it into a solitary religion is to destroy it."

As a reformer, Wesley was far ahead of his time. His social concern was no vague idealism. He had the mind of a capable administrator. He at once formed the converts from his missions into fellowship groups which in time became Christian congregations crystallizing the results of his apostolic work. In so doing—and this of course he could not know—"he began a new chapter in the religious, social, and educational history of the working-class in England."[17] More than anyone else in the eighteenth century Wesley created a taste for good reading and tried to satisfy it with cheap, good literature.

This "concern" was strengthened by his own contact with men and women who had already come under the influence of the mission. He visited them in their homes and found such misery as he never expected to see in his own land: people literally starving for a piece of bread or a man dragging himself out of bed to go to work because otherwise there would be nothing to eat in the house. For Wesley, to see a need was to act. Not only did he rouse the well-to-do members of his society to tackle the problems of relief in their own districts, but right up to the end of his life, whenever he had contact with people in trouble in a certain place, he would go round the town begging for money, clothes, and food. When he was eighty-one, for instance, he went out into the town where he was staying and collected two hundred pounds as well as clothes: "It was hard work," he says, "as most of the streets were filled with melting snow, which often lay ankle deep."[18] Another time when he heard that some French prisoners of war were being ill-treated in a camp outside Bristol, he visited the camp, found terrible neglect and suffering, collected the necessities of life for them, and roused the local authorities to improve the conditions of the camp, which they did without delay. Caring so much for basic human need led Wesley to live on as little as possible. Whatever he earned by his writings beyond the sum he had set aside for his own expenses, he gave away, and when he died he left nothing behind but four silver spoons.

Another evil which he fought all his life was slavery. He had seen something of it at firsthand when he was in Georgia, and the more he heard and read about Negro slavery, the more heavily did this burden of oppression weigh upon his heart and mind. Long before the Committee for the Abolition of Slavery had been formed in 1787, Wesley was protesting publicly against the trade in African slaves.[19] In 1774 he published a small book, *Thoughts on Slavery*, which was a very forceful attack upon the slave trade and had a great influence upon public opinion. Only six days before his death he wrote an encouraging letter to Wilberforce, British antislavery leader, urging him to go on with his efforts for the abolition of the slave trade.[20] Even during his last illness the burden of his suffering "Negro brethren" was heavy on his heart. War was another subject on which Wesley felt strongly. He always denounced war,[21] calling it "a madness and a barbarity." For,

Whenever war breaks out,
God is forgotten.

Among the various portraits of John Wesley none are more striking than those which show him as an old man. We can understand why his eyes riveted the attention of his hearers. He was a small, spare man. He held himself very erect, with an aristocratic bearing which was evidently natural to him. He could look everyone in the face, whether friends or foes. His features were finely chiselled and his expression calm and serene. He undoubtedly had what we now call "a good constitution," for in spite of some illnesses, the amount of sustained work he required of himself must have taxed tremendous energies. He never retired; he simply went on doing the work to which he was called, years after most men would have either given up all active work or died. But he did not waste his strength. He obeyed the laws of health so far as he understood them: he lived frugally; rationed his hours of sleep; rose early; was a great walker in his youth; and traveled thousands of miles on horseback, which meant that he led almost an "open-air" life. He was always punctual; planned his time sensibly; never tried to do more than *he* considered possible in a day (though his companions might have thought differently!); and did not fret or worry. He was very cheerful; his

Journal contains gleams of humor which sparkle here and there in the matter-of-fact record. The very fact that his energy was so unfailing made him sometimes appear hard on others who had not the same good health, a thing quite beyond his understanding: what *he* could do, everyone else could do. He did not seem to realize that in this respect he was different from other people.

Active as ever, in 1783 and 1786 he went over to Holland and greatly enjoyed his visits there. In 1787 he spent four weeks in the Channel Islands. By this time mob violence had long ceased; wherever he went people, old and young alike, were delighted to see and hear him. In 1790 (when he was nearly eighty-seven) he admits that he "begins to feel old."[22] But he still went on traveling about and preaching to large congregations. He never grew stale. His message was always the same, and yet it was always fresh. Each day "called him to a new adventure and was a fresh gift from God." He had not lost the power of moving men's hearts.

His last illness was brief. He died in peace and joy, in the spirit of praise, on the second of March, 1791, in his eighty-eighth year, in City Road, London. Shortly before he died, he said,[23]

The best of all is, God is with us.

WESLEY'S INFLUENCE

Augustine Birrell, in his introduction to the abridged edition of Wesley's *Journal* published in 1902, says that if we want to get into the heart of the eighteenth century in England we should read this *Journal*: "No man lived nearer the centre than John Wesley. Neither Clive nor Pitt, neither Mansfield nor Johnson. You cannot cut him out of our national life. No single figure influenced so many minds, no single voice touched so many hearts. No other man did such a life's work for England."

Such a verdict could be paralleled several times over in the writings of men dealing with the eighteenth century. William Lecky, for instance, a standard writer on this century in England, speaks of Methodism in these terms: "Although the career of the elder Pitt and the splendid victories by land and sea that were won during his ministry form unquestionably the most dazzling episodes in the reign of George II, they must yield, I think, in real importance to that religious revolution which shortly before had begun in England by the preaching of the Wesleys and Whitefield."[24] John R. Green writes: "The Methodists themselves were the least result of the Methodist revival. Its action upon the Church broke the lethargy of the clergy. . . . But the noblest result of the religious revival was the steady attempt . . . from that day to this to remedy the guilt, the ignorance, the physical suffering, the social degradation of the . . . poor."[25] In the opinion of a French historian like Halévy and others it was the Methodist revival, under the influence of John Wesley in particular, which saved England from the horrors of revolution.

Some of the most moving testimonies to the greatness of John Wesley come—rather amazingly—from some modern Roman Catholic writers, both French and English. For instance, John M. Todd, a Catholic layman, says at the end of his book on *John Wesley and the Catholic Church*: "The great men and women, like good trees, are good in themselves all through from root to leaf, and use well the soil in which they grow, to produce a good quantity of very good fruit. John Wesley was such a man."[26]

Most striking of all are the words in which Fr. Maximin Piette ends his great book on *John Wesley in the Evolution of Protestantism*. "John Wesley has been compared to St. Benedict as regards his liturgical sense and piety; to St. Dominic for his apostolic zeal; to St. Francis for his love of Christ and detachment from the world; to St. Ignatius of Loyola for his genius as an organizer."[27]

But here is a final word from a Methodist: Henry

Bett, in *The Spirit of Methodism*, says that the growth of Methodism into a world-wide Christian community is a unique phenomenon in the history of the church, but it is unique in another sense: "it stands in the most intimate connexion with the religious experience of one man."[28]

Wesley's Chapel
City Road, London, England

JOHN WESLEY'S CHRISTIAN PERFECTION

THE ORIGINAL TITLE of this small book is *A Plain Account of Christian Perfection.** It represents the essence of John Wesley's teaching on this subject. But a good deal more can be gathered from his other writings and especially from the hymns of the two Wesley brothers. The *Plain Account* was finally published in 1777, but it sums up what Wesley "believed and taught" about Christian perfection from 1725 to 1777 (p. xi).

Wesley begins by explaining how he was led to formulate this doctrine and shows us how it grew out of his own experience. So we see that this book was not written in a quiet study, away from the happenings of ordinary life, but in the midst of a very full life and in close touch with people of all kinds. This doctrine is no "airy-fairy" theory, but

* All quotations from *Christian Perfection* by John Wesley are identified by the page number on which they appear and have been reprinted by permission of The World Publishing Co. from *Christian Perfection* by John Wesley (c. 1954), edited with an introduction by Thomas S. Kepler.

it is solid teaching based on the Bible and tested by long experience, especially in the lives of the early Methodists.

Wesley begins by stating his aim (p. 3):

> *What I purpose in the following papers is to give a plain and distinct account of the steps by which I was led, during a course of many years, to embrace the doctrine of Christian perfection.*

He says that he wants to show "serious" people "both what I thought, and why I thought so."

The first book which stirred his interest and desire was a small but famous book by Jeremy Taylor (1613-1667), usually known as *Holy Living and Holy Dying*. Taylor was born and educated in Cambridge, England; during the Civil War he was a chaplain in the Royalist army. After a short period of imprisonment, he went to live in Wales for some years where he wrote most of his best books. Later he became a bishop in Ireland. *Holy Living and Holy Dying* has become a classic, both for its content and its style. It made such a deep impression on Wesley that he instantly resolved (p. 3)

> *to dedicate all my life to God.*

The following year (when John was twenty-four) he came across the still more celebrated book by Thomas á Kempis entitled *The Imitation of Christ.* Thomas á Kempis lived from 1380 to 1471; he lived quietly in a monastery in Holland and was greatly valued as a spiritual adviser. His book has world-wide fame and still speaks to the hearts of people in many lands and many tongues. After the Bible, it is believed to be the most widely read Christian book. Wesley then began to see more deeply into the purpose of God's call: he saw that God wanted his *heart*, as well as his *life*, and indeed (p. 4)

> *I saw that giving even all my life to God (supposing it possible to do this, and go no further) would profit me nothing unless I gave my heart, yea, all my heart to him.*

. . . all my life to God . . .
all my heart to him . . .

. . . my God and my all. . . .

WHOLENESS
HOLINESS
PERFECTION

With his thoughts and desires already reaching out after holiness, a year or two later he was much moved by two books by William Law: *Christian Perfection* and *A Serious Call to a Devout and Holy Life*. William Law was also a noted spiritual writer: he lived from 1686 to 1761, so that he was a contemporary of Wesley's. Law himself had been influenced by Thomas á Kempis and many other earlier writers. He remained an Anglican, though in later years he held views very like those of the Quakers. It is interesting to see what Wesley says about the impression these books made upon him. They convinced him more than ever of (p. 4)

the absolute impossibility
of being half a Christian.

More and more he was being led to see that "holiness" means "wholeness": being a *whole* person.

Having been so deeply stirred and influenced by these spiritual classics, Wesley now began to study the subject of "perfection," or "sanctification," in the Bible itself (p. 5):

> *Hence I saw in a clearer and clearer light the indispensable necessity of having "the mind which was in Christ" . . .*
>
> *At this time I generally considered religion, as a uniform following of Christ, an entire inward and outward conformity to our Master.*

This reminds us of our Lord's own words: "If therefore thine eye be single, thy whole body [or personality] shall be full of light" (Matt. 6:22). By 1733, Wesley's thought had matured to such an extent that, when he was asked to preach in the university Church of St. Mary's at Oxford, on New Year's Day, he chose as his subject "The Circumcision of the Heart" and dwelt on the necessity for "wholeness—holiness—perfection." He declared (pp. 5-6):

> *Love is the fulfilling of the law,*
> *the end of the commandment.*

In the beginning of the year 1738 the cry of his heart was (pp. 8-9):

O grant that nothing in my soul
May dwell, but Thy pure love alone!
O may Thy love possess me whole,
My joy, my treasure, and my crown!
Strange fires far from my heart remove;
My every act, word, thought, be love!

It is curious that in this year which was to bring the "heart-warming experience" of May 24, he does not even mention it in *Christian Perfection*, but goes straight on to August of the same year, where he speaks of his meeting with a German friend which helped him a great deal—confirming what he had been thinking for some time past. After this, as we can see, much of this new thought and experience comes out in the various collections of hymns which were written and published by himself and his brother Charles (pp. 25 and 33). In the first tract he wrote on this subject he speaks of this perfection as *perfect love*. The words of this tract from which he quotes are very rich and moving, and he sums up the heart of this little work by saying (pp. 16-17): "These are the very words wherein I largely declared, for the first time, my sentiments of Christian perfection," and adds that, since then, for thirty-eight years, he has never taught anything else.

The sections of this book in which Wesley sums up the findings of various Conferences on the subject of perfection need to be studied carefully (pp. 41-49, 53-75). At first they may seem rather dry, but as we try to enter into the spirit of these discussions we begin to feel the deep desire for *truth* which lies behind them. Perhaps for some people the best way to grasp what these men were talking about is to put these conversations into the language of the present day.

. . . *holiness means wholeness* . . .

. . . my every act, word, thought be love!

WHAT DID WESLEY MEAN BY PERFECTION?

In this account of the way in which Wesley came to think about the subject of perfection, as we have seen, there is one strange omission: why does he say nothing about his great experience at Aldersgate? Why? Traditional Methodist teaching has always laid a great deal of stress upon this event; and doubtless this is right. But sometimes this view has been challenged; some people go so far as to call it a "legend."

Dr. Sangster, in his book *The Path to Perfection*, insists that whatever it was that Wesley received on that day, and in that particular experience, it was a turning point in his life. For years Wesley had been seeking for a deeper spiritual life; and as we know, he was already resolved to be fully dedicated to God. And still he was hungry and unsatisfied. On the twenty-fourth of May, suddenly and very quietly, everything, as it were, fell into place. What seems to have happened on that memorable day was this: the holiness he had been trying to achieve by his own efforts he now saw could only be received by faith. In this flash of illumination he saw that "God can do more with sin than forgive it: He can destroy it. . . . The effort to make oneself holy is useless. . . . By faith God will work a perfect cure."[29] The days of sad introspection were over. Henceforth all Wesley's attention was turned away from self: upward to God in thanksgiving and trust, outward to man in loving service.

In all his teaching on holiness it is evident that Wesley was concerned for *truth*, and for that alone, and in his personal search for holiness he had found a great deal of help in Roman Catholic and Anglican writers. Thus his thought on this subject contains both Catholic and Protestant elements. The result was that Wesley brought back to Protestantism something which it had lost: an urgent concern for holiness.

In his thought, however, as Dr. Sangster points out, "He seems not to have allowed enough for the difference between a changed relation with God and a completely changed life."[30] In his writings he seems to hover between the ideas of *perfection as given in an instant*, and *perfection as a growth*. He is not always very clear or consistent in the way he speaks about this, but in one place he says plainly (also see pp. 68, 104-105):

> *You don't* GROW INTO *it:*
> *you are* BORN INTO *it, and you* GROW IN *it.*

This is a statement which most of us could understand and accept.

Again, Wesley speaks of this "sanctified" life sometimes as though it were a permanent state, and sometimes as a life received moment-by-moment, in utter dependence upon God. This is not so contradictory as it sounds. We might say the same about the practice of prayer: in a way it is a state which lasts all the time, whether we are aware of it or not, as long as our hearts are set on doing the will of God in everything; on the other hand, prayer is also an activity, and moment by moment we receive fresh life from God as we turn to him in times set apart for prayer, whether they are short or long.

Wesley himself was not quite happy about the title, *Christian Perfection*: he wanted to drop it. Even in his lifetime some of his friends used to be amused by it, which shows that it was not acceptable, even then. A better phrase, he thought, which he used now and again, would be "perfect love."

Dr. R. Newton Flew, another eminent Methodist writer, sums up the main points in Wesley's teaching on perfection thus:[31]

1. *The necessity of aiming at perfection.* He saw that every part of his life must be dedicated to God.
2. *This perfection is love* [in the deepest and widest sense].
3. *Love includes the keeping of all the commandments* [of God].
4. *Perfection is freedom from sin.* [By sin Wesley evidently means a falling short of the divine ideal for humanity or . . . a voluntary transgression of a known law of God.]
5. *Distinction between voluntary and involuntary transgressions.* [Dr. Flew says that apparently Wesley deliberately avoided this distinction but that by 1759] the distinction between sin as the voluntary transgression of a known law and sin as the involuntary transgression of a divine law, known or unknown, is clearly stated as part of the doctrine which the Methodists believed.
6. *The reception of the experience* [sanctification] *is instantaneous.* [But work leads to and follows the instant.]

7. *The Assurance of the Great Salvation.* [Wesley nowhere claims the experience he so often described.]

Its main weakness, Dr. Flew holds, seems to be a defective view of sin. This seems strange in a man who was such a wonderful preacher, with a strong sense of the love of Christ for sinners, and such a power of bringing this home to thousands. For instance, it is curious that he scarcely mentions the sins of omission, which are such a terrible part of the burden of sin of which we have to repent. When Wesley speaks of sin in connection with holiness, he speaks of it as if it were an evil growth which could be cut out as a whole; here there is no sense of the pervading character of sin, which is more like a poisonous weed so deeply entangled with the roots of our being that it seems impossible to do more than cut it back; nothing but a long exposure to the divine Light will allow the healing grace of God to get through to the roots. The greatest saints have known and admitted that they were sinners to the end. St. Teresa of Avila, for instance, who had experienced so much of the love of God in her own life, died with the words of the fifty-first Psalm on her lips: "Create in me a clean heart, O God."

At the same time, it is possible that John Wesley

did not always express himself clearly on this point; so it may be unjust to say that his view of sin is defective. In any case, those of his followers who exaggerated his teaching and claimed that he taught the possibility of "sinless perfection" are certainly mistaken. Wesley himself says plainly (p. 22):

A Christian is so far perfect
as not to commit sin.

But in his *Letters* we find,[32]

Absolute and infallible PERFECTION*?*
I never contended for it.
SINLESS PERFECTION*?*
Neither do I contend for this,
seeing the term is not scriptural.

Wesley's positive ideal of the meaning of holiness is summed up in words which speak to the heart: "This it is to be a perfect man . . . 'to have a heart so all-flaming with the love of God' (to use Archbishop Usher's words) 'as continually to offer up every thought, word, and work as a spiritual sacrifice, acceptable to God through Christ.'" "This," he says, "is the doctrine which we preached from the beginning and which we preach at this day" (p. 36). This reminds us of his brother's hymn:[33]

> O Thou who camest from above,
> The pure celestial fire t' impart,
> Kindle a flame of sacred love
> On the mean altar of my heart.

. . . Beware of sins of omission; lose no opportunity of doing good in any kind . . .

. . . such light and strength . . .

WESLEY'S PERSONAL EXPERIENCE

St. François de Sales, in the Preface to his famous book, *Introduction to the Devout Life,* says at one point: "It is true, dear reader, that here I write of a devout life without being devout myself. Yet it is certainly not without a desire of becoming so, and it is this affection for devotion that encourages me to instruct you."[34] I think we may assume that John Wesley wrote on Christian perfection in the same spirit: he urged the call to holiness because to him it was one of the most important things in life; but, like St. Paul, he never claimed that he, personally, had attained entire sanctification although he often asserted that a great many Methodists *had* received this gift.[35]

He is reticent about his own inner life, but there is one passage in the *Journal* which suggests a growth in self-knowledge through temptation and difficulty . . . a matter of growth which was not "achieved" but "given." On one special occasion he wrote in his *Journal*:[36]

> *I found such light and strength as I never remember to have had before.*
>
> *I saw every thought, as well as action or word, just as it was rising in my heart; and whether it was right before God, or tainted with pride or selfishness.*

Behind this secret growth in self-knowledge lay the profound desire expressed in his brother's lines:[37]

> He wills that I should holy be:
> That holiness I long to feel,
> That full divine conformity
> To all my Saviour's righteous will.

. . . obedience to the law of Christ . . .

APOSTOLIC ZEAL
UNTIRING CHARITY
SELF-DISCIPLINE

John Wesley's apostolic zeal, his untiring charity, prove the reality of his dedication. But behind this lay a lifelong habit of self-discipline. From the days of the Holy Club to the end of his long and fruitful life, John Wesley was a disciplined man. The aim of this discipline was positive, not negative: Wesley practiced self-denial in very ordinary matters in order that he might be free for God to use him. At one time he fasted every Wednesday and Friday until after three in the afternoon. He did his immense work on six hours' sleep every night: from 10 P.M. till 4 A.M. He was scrupulous in the use of time, reserving regular prolonged times for prayer and making the best use of every moment, even when traveling on horseback or waiting for a ship to sail; always he had some work on hand—

writing or study or translation. It is indeed a miracle that he could write so much and earn so much money to give away, when he was incessantly on the move, but in this—as in other matters—nothing was left to chance. He planned the use of everything he had—time, money, and the rest—in order that his whole life might be at the service of his Lord.[38] (Compare pp. 109-110, 119.)

> *Beware of self-indulgence; yea, and making a virtue of it, laughing at self-denial, and [at] taking up the cross daily, at fasting or abstinence.*

Thus there is no doubt about the reality of Wesley's devotion. His whole life proves it. But since he did not claim to be "perfect," *we* ought not to be surprised to find that even he had some defects. In his relations with women, for instance, he was both foolish and unfortunate. The plain truth seems to be that he did not understand either himself or them. Why he made a disastrous marriage with a difficult widow is a mystery. It is a sad story and caused them both a great deal of unhappiness and suffering. But even after his wife had left him, she still thought of him with affection, and in her will she left him a gold ring, "in token that I die in love and friendship towards him." In other ways, too, Wesley was often less than wise in his dealing with people who came to him for help. With his openness to all kinds of human need, he was often duped by clever scoundrels. Charles Wesley once said about John: "My brother was, I think, born for the benefit of knaves."[39]

Others have complained of his "autocratic" behavior. He may have been an autocrat, but could we not say the same about a great many of the outstanding men and women who have been leaders and creators? In any case, the love and peace and joy of his later years show that much of his prayer for love had been answered, for the love of God shone through him up to the last moment when he struggled to sing the praises of God who had called him out of darkness into his marvelous light.

A modern Methodist writer says frankly: "If ever there was a man in this world who deserved to be venerated as a saint, Wesley was one, yet he has not been generally been regarded in that light."[40]

Wesley's other name for perfection was "perfect love" (pp. 116-117)

> *. . . love is the highest gift of God, humble, gentle, patient love; . . . the heaven of heavens is love.*

> *Settle it then in your heart that from the moment God has saved you from all sin, you are to aim at nothing more but more of that love described in the thirteenth chapter of the Corinthians.*

When he speaks like this we may well ask ourselves, what was it in his preaching that broke hardened men's hearts and opened them to the love of God but simply this love pouring through Wesley as he spoke to thousands! What power enabled him to go on preaching and working almost to the last moment of his life but the power of divine love urging him on and giving him the fire and force he needed? "It is not in normal nature to love like that: it is a *given love;* [he had] sought and received [it] from God," and was himself "consumed by its scorching flame."[41] But all this, Wesley knew, was but a foretaste of what was to come. In the words of Charles Wesley:

> Yet when the work is done,
> The work is but begun:
> Partaker of Thy grace,
> I long to see Thy face:
> The first I prove below,
> The last I die to know.

. . . *be exemplary in all things* . . .

DANGERS IN THE DOCTRINE OF PERFECTION

Wesley was well aware of the dangers that attended his teaching on perfection for sometimes it was misunderstood or exaggerated during his lifetime, as well as later. Wesley warns us against some of these dangers.

One of the first is "enthusiasm." Here he used the word in the eighteenth-century sense. He did not mean what we mean nowadays by this term. Then it meant a fanatical and unbalanced zeal . . . extravagance and excitement in religious matters, leading too often to delusions, springing from an overheated imagination. Wesley tried, wisely and firmly, to deal with such phenomena which frequently occur in a religious awakening. (See pp. 75-76, 114, 117; also p. 111, "false zeal.")

Wesley firmly points out the other dangers allied to this spirit of false zeal as pride, self-righteousness, censoriousness leading to disunity in the church and among Christian brethren. Finally, he warns his readers against two other perils (pp. 117-120):

SOLIFIDIANISM: the doctrine that faith alone is necessary for justification, no "works" being needed (on which the Epistle of James speaks so strongly). Wesley admonishes Methodists thus:

> *Our call is to declare the whole counsel of God and to prophesy according to the analogy of faith. The written Word treats of the whole and every particular branch of righteousness, descending to its minutest branches: as to be sober, courteous, diligent, patient, to honor all men.*
>
> *. . . as "by works faith is made perfect," so the completing or destroying the work of faith, and enjoying the favor or suffering the displeasure of God, greatly depends on every single act of obedience or disobedience. . . . Beware of desiring anything but God.*

ANTINOMIANISM: a general term for the view that Christians are by grace set free from observing any moral law—a doctrine which has often worked havoc in the life of the church and is indeed a deadly danger to all Christian life. In answer to this doctrine Wesley says (p. 118):

> *Let this be our voice:*
> *"I prize Thy commandments above gold or precious stones. O, what love have I unto Thy law! all the day long is my study in it."*

Some modern "holiness movements" exaggerate or misinterpret Wesley's teachings and are sometimes described as "Perfectionism." It is important to note that this perfectionist tendency has appeared repeatedly in the course of church history, long before the eighteenth century. For instance, there were the Beghards in the Netherlands in the twelfth century. The movement to which they belonged sprang out of a revival, and its aims were high and pure. But some of the members fell into the error of thinking they were perfect and claiming that "actions normally regarded as sinful are not sinful in the perfect." They then threw off all restraints; men and women lived together and practiced nudism. In the sixteenth century, again, among the Anabaptists there was a sect which called itself " 'the holy and Sinless Baptists,' who claimed that the soul was not responsible (in given circumstances) for the sins of the body."[42]

In the nineteenth century, in the United States as well as elsewhere, this tendency often reappeared. These errors were all the more difficult to deal with because they grew up in circles where there was no external authority to deal with them unless they actually broke the moral law. A wise and devout Quaker woman, Mrs. Whitall Smith, was well aware of these dangers and tried to warn against them. She often met and talked with such people. Of one man—who had gone very far astray—she said: "One of the most saintly men I ever met. . . . Never was there a saintlier man to begin with, and never was there a more pitiful fall. . . . All the fanatics I have ever known have been at the same time the most devoted of Christians, and have fallen into their fanaticisms along the paths of the most entire consecration to the Lord, and the most absolute faith in His guidance." Such people always said to her, when she tried to reason with them, "But, Mrs. Smith, what *am* I to do? These inward voices come to me in my most solemn and sacred moments."[43]

Why do such things happen? The longing for holiness is divinely implanted. Where then do we go wrong? Usually because on some vital point we become fanatical, or one-sided, or unbalanced. This means that we have separated what God has joined together. Holiness is "wholeness," and we have no right to sever ourselves from the visible church in excessive individualism, nor to speak and think and act as if the soul were severed from the body. It is the whole personality which is to be consecrated to God.

. . . to declare
the whole counsel of God . . .

. . . a heart and life all
devoted to God . . .

WESLEY'S TEACHING TODAY

There is another point in Wesley's teaching which does not directly come under the head of perfection yet we must note it in passing: that of "assurance." So far as this simply means a strong faith in Christ, it is quite clear that it is a central element in the Christian life as a whole. But in his earlier days Wesley went further and taught[44]

> *. . . righteousness, peace and joy in the Holy Ghost. These must be* felt, *or they have no being. All therefore who condemn inward feelings in the gross, leave no place either for joy, peace, or love in religion; and . . . reduce it to a dry, dead carcass.*

And he certainly thought that *feeling* was most important. Many years later, however, when he was sitting alone in a coach traveling from Newmarket to Norwich, he was thinking deeply on this subject, and then he saw that there was "value in that conception of faith which holds the feelings to be something quite beside the mark."[45] He even went so far as to say that he thought that "full assurance"[46] was not granted to many people.

Here then, in the end, Fénelon and Wesley meet. Their teaching on this subject is as relevant as ever for untold harm and unhappiness is caused by too great an emphasis upon feeling in the spiritual life. To learn to turn our eyes away from ourselves and to rejoice in God because he is what *he* is and to thank him for all *his* love and goodness is an exercise in a living faith. It was in this spirit that both these great men lived.

In his *Journal* for June 27, 1769, Wesley puts down a few sentences from a letter he had been writing "to a pious and sensible woman" on the subject of Christian perfection. Evidently she had been asking his advice. In it he says:[47]

> *By Christian Perfection I mean: Loving God with all our heart . . . a heart and life all devoted to God . . . Having all the mind that was in Christ . . . Walking uniformly as Christ walked. And this surely no Christian will object to.*

How *right* Wesley was to lay so much stress on holiness. At the present time most of us would agree that far too many Christians live on a sub-Christian level. What people used to call "the Higher Life," and the like, was only a reminder of the New Testament level, which is the normal Christian life; so much of our present experience and practice is subnormal, if not sometimes abnormal. Dr. Sangster says that "the gait [of many Christians is] so waddling, and the journey so undirected that, as has been remarked, they seem more like penguins than pilgrims."[48] And he goes on to urge upon us the need for a much more realistic faith. For "God is able, and willing, and eager, to deal drastically with sin in us, the sins of the mind as well as the sins of the flesh, the jealousies, pettinesses, irritabilities, resentments, egotisms"[49] which tie us down to a low level of Christian living.

"Yet the way is open for all. Holiness is not a monopoly of the cloisters, or of one branch of Christendom. The energies of the Holy Spirit are available to everyone who will seek Him."[50]

Evelyn Underhill

and

THE SPIRITUAL LIFE

EVELYN UNDERHILL

London is a city of surprises. In many districts it is still possible to step in a moment out of the noise of a great thoroughfare into a quiet oasis of peace belonging to an earlier age. Kensington has several oases of this kind. It still bears the distinctive name of the "Royal Borough," because at the end of the seventeenth century William III chose to live there at Kensington Palace. Until that time Kensington, though already old, had been little more than a village. At once it became fashionable. Many great houses were built there in large shady gardens, and it still bears the traces of those spacious days. Campden Hill Square, where Evelyn Underhill lived for the greater part of her life, is a square (or three sides of one) built round a beautiful garden, full of trees and grass and flowers. It opens off a great main road running out to the West. The houses are full of character; most of them date from the eighteenth century—so they must have been there in the days of Wesley. The whole Square is built upon a low but rather steep little hill, and from the upper windows of the larger houses there is a grand view of London, both towards the East and the West. This Campden Hill district is still one of the pleasantest parts of London. No. 50 has no sign of the occupancy of its former mistress, but the house is practically unchanged, and the whole Square is as quiet and beautiful as ever. Evelyn Underhill loved the country, but she had to live in the town. It was here in a small house with a very rural garden at the back that she lived in time and in sight of Eternity.

Her early poem *Uxbridge Road* suggests how she lived in two worlds at once: the seen and the unseen. Evidently these verses express an experience which came to her when she was walking along the noisy thoroughfare which sweeps past the bottom of Campden Hill:[1]

The Western Road goes streaming out to seek the cleanly wild,
It pours the city's dim desires towards the undefiled,

. . . .

The torments of that seething tide who is there that can see?
There's one who walked with starry feet the western road by me!

. . . .

He drives them east, he drives them west, between the dark and light;
He pastures them in city pens, he leads them home at night.
The towery trams, the threaded trains, like shuttles to and fro
To weave the web of working days in ceaseless travel go.

. . . .

Behold! he lent me as we went the vision of the seer;
Behold! I saw the life of men, the life of God shine clear.
I saw the hidden Spirit's thrust; I saw the race fulfil
The spiral of its steep ascent, predestined of the Will.
Yet not unled, but shepherded by one they may not see—
The one who walked with starry feet the western road by me.

WHO WAS EVELYN UNDERHILL?

In our two previous studies we have been learning about Christian perfection, or holiness, from two great men of the seventeenth and the eighteenth centuries. Evelyn Underhill lived in an eighteenth-century background, but she belongs to the latter part of the nineteenth century and to nearly the whole of the first half of the twentieth century. The fact that her books are still being reissued and are widely read shows that she speaks to our own day. It is a striking fact that, though Fénelon has been chosen to represent the seventeenth-century search for perfection, and Wesley, the eighteenth, it is to a *woman* that we turn for our own day. Moreover, she was a woman who never sought fame or publicity. She was content to work quietly and unobtrusively, but her gifts could not be hid. Obviously she was an exceptional person.

But when we say this it may suggest a person who is peculiar, if not eccentric; unusual to a degree which one might admire at a distance, but not the sort of person it would be easy to know; possibly someone rather frightening. To many people who have only read her books, or some of them, she may be a revered figure, but rather like a figure in a stained-glass window.

Friedrich von Hügel, writing to a friend, has some wise remarks on this subject. He says that the "exceptional" person is never "queer" but is, on the contrary, "supremely normal." He thinks that this is due to the fact that at bottom all men are moved by desires and aspirations after something higher and better than themselves, though they may start at a very low or primitive level. Thus the "saint" is the "exceptional" person in whom these confused longings have become clarified, purified, and deepened, because they are fulfilled in God. This was certainly true of Evelyn Underhill: she was exceptional, and she was supremely normal; as someone has said: she was a "great saint and a great human being." She does not fall into any category. She was not like anyone else, even on her own high plane. She was simply *herself*: a many-sided, witty, lovable, delightful, and fascinating person, who touched life at many points and *cared greatly* for people.

Yet there was a reticence and a mystery about her which meant that, like so many other people, she could never reveal herself fully to another human being. She was "at home" only in God. That is why no biography of her can be entirely satisfactory. Something always eludes us. The nearest we can get to her now is through her own writings, which are many and are addressed to all sorts of people. But it may help us to get a more balanced view if we know something about the life she lived and what she was like to her friends and to the many whom she served with so much love and care.

Anyone who reads her larger books realizes at once the wealth of learning and the brilliance of intellect which lie behind them. She had great abilities and gifts, not least the clarity and honesty of her mind and her love of truth. The breadth and depth of her outlook was due to the fact that her spiritual and her intellectual faculties were truly integrated under the creative action of God through a long, hidden training which was sometimes very hard and painful.

She wrote and spoke with authority because she knew what she was talking about. In her writings theology comes alive, for her one subject was God: God himself, in his majesty, greatness, and glory. On the mantelpiece of her study in Campden Hill Square there stood an embroidered panel containing the one word—ever before her eyes as she worked and wrote—Eternity. She saw all life in this light. That is why she lays so much stress on the *priority* of God, that is, on the fact that he always comes first; he begins, he originates, everything; apart from him we would fade out; there would be nothing left. He is All. That, too, is why she constantly urges us to look away from ourselves to God, to worship and adore him, and then to turn to the world and its need, and accept the humblest tasks in the service of his kingdom. In one of her later books, *Abba*, a study of the Lord's Prayer, she says:[3]

> *Glory is the final word of religion, as joy is its final state. The sparks and trickles of the Supernatural which come to us, the hints received through beauty and through sacrifice . . . all these are earnests of a Perfection, a Wholeness yet unseen: as the small range of sound and colour revealed by the senses witness to the unseen colour and unheard music of a Reality which lies beyond their narrow span.*
>
> *Behind every closed door which seems to shut experience from us He is standing; and within every experience which reaches us, however disconcerting, His unchanging presence is concealed.*
>
> *In the "voice of gentle stillness" speaking from within the agony and bewilderment of life, we recognize the presence of the Holy and the completing answer to the*

soul's completed prayer . . . in Thine unchanging quiet is our trust.

All who came into real contact with Evelyn Underhill felt—though possibly they would not have been able to say why—that they were in the presence of someone who "stood within the frontiers of Eternity." One was very conscious of that in her company. She herself often said,[4]

> *It is not Christian to leave the mystery out. Christ does not leave it out; His teaching has a deep note of awe, a solemn sense of God and the profound mystery of God. . . .*
>
> *His teaching all ends in one thing,* GOD, *who is greater than our heart. Once we have learnt that lesson, all else falls into place.*

HER LIFE

The outward story of her life is soon told. It was not spectacular. Its drama and intensity, as we shall see, lay out of sight.

Evelyn Underhill was born at Wolverhampton on the eighth of December, 1875, and she died in

1941. Her father, Arthur Underhill, was a solicitor at the time of his daughter's birth. About that time he decided to become a barrister; and for that reason he moved with his family to London. For the first ten years he had a hard struggle to establish himself. Later he rose high in his profession and was well known as Sir Arthur Underhill. Evelyn Underhill was very close to her mother, and as she grew older she shared her father's interest in the law as well as his passion for the sea. All through her life she was a loyal, affectionate daughter and remained in close touch with her parents, though she was a married woman long before they grew old.

She was educated partly in London, but mainly at a boarding school at Folkestone, on the coast of Kent, in sight of France in clear weather. When she came home at the age of sixteen, she went to King's College (University of London) for various courses in botany and modern languages and later in social science and philosophy. Evelyn was always efficient in everything she undertook; she never played about with things. She showed her literary bent very early and wrote a great deal before she had any idea of becoming a professional writer.

Evelyn was an only child. She might have had a lonely childhood, but fortunately for her, her parents were intimate with a family in their neighborhood where there were several boys. Their mother had died while they were all young, so Mrs. Underhill welcomed the friendship between the two families for the sake of the children. Evelyn grew up with these boys, who were like her own brothers. Later, with one of them, friendship ripened into love and later into marriage.

One of the great joys of her life was foreign travel. She first went abroad, to France, at the age of fifteen. From 1898 onwards every spring she went to the Continent with her mother, mainly to France, Switzerland, and Italy. After her first visit to Florence she wrote to a friend: "This place has taught me more than I can tell you; it's a sort of gradual unconscious growing into an understanding of things."[5] Here she was alluding to the profound impression made upon her by Italian religious art. This experience of western Europe greatly enlarged her outlook on life. Never again could her viewpoint be narrow. Speaking French and Italian fluently, she was able to enter to some extent into the lives of the people she met. When she was only seventeen she wrote for her own guidance these words:[6]

> *I hope my mind will not grow tall to look down on things but wide to embrace all sorts of things during the coming year.*

On this Charles Williams remarks: "Many girls at seventeen might have aspired so; some might have succeeded. What was remarkable about Evelyn Underhill was that, during the next few years, she not only 'embraced' friends; she saw and 'embraced' Europe."[7] Not only did she glory in the splendor of mountains—they always meant a great deal to her—but the impressions she received from Italian art touched some spring within her which had never been touched before. As she looked slowly and broodingly at the paintings she was penetrated by something strange and yet perturbing: she felt the presence of what she called "the Beyond." Later she expressed this in a novel in which one of the characters describes a picture portraying "The Madonna adoring the Infant Christ":[8]

> *As he watched her something unearthly, something remote from life laid its quieting hand upon him. These things had not been conceived in the petty agitations of ordinary life. The Beyond had been at their birth, and left a token of its presence.*

Italy, and above all Umbria, came to mean a very great deal to her, with its blending of natural beauty, fine architecture, art, and history. But it was mainly the *spirit* it breathed, especially in holy places like Assisi, that attracted her most. In another novel she writes:[9]

> *In Umbria, clothed with olive woods where Francis walked . . . there is a Peace of God eternally established. In this country . . . spirits wearied by dark journeyings may still feel the quieting touch of Immanent Peace.*

Other holidays were spent in sailing which was a delight she shared with her parents and with Hubert her future husband. One of her early poems is full of a youthful delight in the joy of sailing, "dancing down the Channel with the breeze."[10]

The year 1902 was an important one for her. About this time Mrs. Underhill accepted the fact that Evelyn and Hubert would eventually marry, though for some unexplained reason this did not take place till 1907. During these years Evelyn Underhill was beginning her career as a writer. A small book of amusing verse was followed by two novels and then by a beautiful translation of a medieval book of tales which revealed her scholarship and her linguistic ability.

A friend who met her about this time tells us

what she remembers of her in her youth. She speaks of her friendship "with a delightful being who stands out fondly in the memories of my youth. She was gentle, quiet and unassuming . . . exceedingly modest, and never spoke of herself or of her writing."[11] In 1907 Evelyn and Hubert were married, and she went to live in his house at 50 Campden Hill Square. After she had settled down, she took up her writing again with renewed zest. It was during these early years of married life that she wrote her famous book on *Mysticism*. These years (between 1907 and 1914) were busy, happy, and quiet. Though she never sought fame, her reputation as an outstanding author and poet was growing. She and her husband—who was a lawyer, like her father—had a great many common interests and a lively circle of friends. As her reputation increased, Hubert became very proud of her.

The outbreak of war in 1914 was a great shock. At that time Evelyn was not a pacifist, but she was greatly troubled by the whole moral question of war. For a time she went on as usual, then she evidently felt that she ought to do something definite which could be called "war work." She applied to the Admiralty where her languages were needed, and she translated books and documents for them. A friend who worked with her and came to know her in 1916 gives a vivid description of her at that time: "The astonishing thing about Evelyn in 1916 when I first met her, and when she was already a very well-known and respected poet and writer, was her gaiety. She was not certainly an impressive or even a striking object at first sight. She was smallish, stooping, and round-shouldered, her clothes definitely dowdy and her hair most unsatisfactory . . . but her . . . face was an instant attraction . . . always creased with laughter and twinkling with fun."[12] This friend says that she had expected to meet someone rather "exquisitely withdrawn" and remote, but instead she met a woman who was natural, approachable, and full of fun: "It was most refreshing." This same friend says that she often went to Evelyn's home and that they talked about everything, perhaps chiefly, however, about philosophy, psychology, and religion.

At the end of the war, in 1918, Evelyn was more than a writer. She was now well known as a religious writer of eminence. But underneath she was not satisfied. Something seemed to be missing. She wrote to von Hügel: "During the war I went to pieces."[13] And in her distress she asked him to come to her aid. She had known him from 1911. In 1921 she asked him to direct her spiritual development.

HER SPIRITUAL DEVELOPMENT

At this point we must retrace our steps. We cannot understand the Evelyn Underhill of the later years unless we know how she came to be what she was. To do this we have to trace—as far as that is possible—the story of her spiritual development.

Looking back to her childhood, Evelyn Underhill says frankly, "I was not brought up to religion." Her parents were not churchgoers. Her father said he had had too much of "school-chapels" as a boy; possibly he did not meet the right sort of people while he was young. They were not hostile to religion, but it did not count for much in their lives. At boarding school, however, Evelyn had a good deal of it, and she seems to have accepted it all as it came. Indeed, she took her Confirmation (at school) and her First Communion very seriously. Later on, however, this religious interest faded, and for a time she was practically an agnostic. But, as we have seen, Italian art and the churches she visited in France and Italy, as well as in her own country, aroused a latent thirst for something more.

Gradually, she began to be aware that what she calls "the Christian net" was closing round her. She felt herself being drawn, gradually but very surely, towards God, through the Roman Catholic

Church. While she was staying in a convent with a friend, she became deeply convinced of the truth of the Christian faith. She says:

"I was 'converted' quite suddenly [from agnosticism], once for all, by an overpowering vision which had really no specifically Christian elements, but yet convinced me that the Catholic religion was true."[14] She was so strongly attracted that she went forward with inquiries and interviews and had almost decided to become a Catholic when something happened which altered the whole situation.

On the third of July, 1906, she had announced her engagement to Hubert Stuart Moore; and they were to be married in 1907. Of course she now told Hubert all that was going on in her mind. He was very troubled by the prospect of her becoming a Catholic and asked her to put it off for six months. This she at once agreed to do. While she was waiting, the Church of Rome made some public statements about Modernism which made her realize that she could never accept membership in this church and preserve her intellectual freedom and honesty. She saw that she could not possibly go forward along this path, much as she wanted to do so. So she gave up the idea, and was married to Hubert Stuart Moore on July 3, 1907.

It was during this time of inward strain and

searching that she began to study the lives of the saints and mystics in preparation for her book, *Mysticism.* When this book was published it made a great stir, and it made her name as a religious writer. In later life she said publicly that there was a good deal in this book which she would have liked to alter. But the book shows very clearly that here is someone whose soul is athirst for the living God. Nothing less would ever satisfy her. She had become increasingly aware of the silent but insistent working of the Spirit of God not only in the lives of the saints about whom she wrote, but in her own life as well. On the fifteenth of May, 1911, she wrote:[15]

> *But I cling to St. Paul. . . . Is it not amazing when one can . . . see the action of the Spirit of God: so gentle, ceaseless, inexorable, pressing you bit by bit whether you like it or not towards your home? I feel this more and more as the dominating thing—it seems so odd that everyone does not feel and notice it happening. . . .*

From 1911 onwards her life falls into two clear parts which are divided by the death of Baron von Hügel in 1925. It was his influence which meant more than anything else in her life: as we have already said, from 1911 to 1921 she knew him as a friend. In 1921 she asked him to guide her in her spiritual life. He died in 1925. Here again, as we saw with Fénelon and with Wesley WHEN A PERSON IS IN GREAT NEED, AND IN DESPERATE EARNESTNESS IN THE SEARCH FOR GOD, THE HELP NEEDED COMES AT THE RIGHT MOMENT. Fénelon met Madame Guyon; Wesley met Peter Böhler; at the turning point in her life, Evelyn Underhill met Friedrich von Hügel.*

This period (1921-1924) was the central point in her life. All that went before had led up to it. It came to a climax in a period of four months (1923-1924). Afterwards her way was plain before her. She had "come into her own."†

In a letter written to an intimate friend about 1927 she gives her own account of this experience.[16]

> *Until about five years ago I had never had* ANY *personal experience of our Lord. I*

*Baron Friedrich von Hügel (1852-1925) was a liberal Roman Catholic (lay) theologian and philosopher. His father was an Austrian nobleman, and his mother a Scottish Presbyterian who had become a Roman Catholic. After a continental education he came to England and lived in London. His religious influence was great, especially outside his own communion.

† In 1954 I was privileged to read the whole of this correspondence between von Hügel and Evelyn Underhill (for 1923-1924). For some time these letters seemed hopelessly lost. But almost miraculously they were recovered just before being thrown away as so much waste paper.

> *didn't know what it meant. I was a convinced theocentric, . . . This position I thought to be that of a broadminded and intelligent Christian, but when . . . I went to the Baron . . . he said I wasn't much better than a Unitarian! Somehow by his prayers or something he* COMPELLED *me to experience Christ. He never said anything more about it—but I know humanly speaking he did it. It took about four months—it was like watching the sun rise very slowly —and then suddenly one knew what it was.*

For some years after this she moved slowly in her new life, but she found herself more and more drawn towards Christ:[17]

> *I seem to have to try as it were to live more and more towards Him only . . . The New Testament, which once I couldn't make much of or meditate on, now seems full of things never noticed—all gets more and* MORE *alive and compelling and beautiful . . . Holy Communion, which at first I did simply under obedience, gets more and more wonderful too. It's in that world and atmosphere one lives.*

This great inward change bore fruit throughout the rest of her life. As we know she already had done a great deal and was a well-known religious writer. From this time forward her life ran in a deeper channel and at the same time brought her into a great deal of public work. Increasingly, she was asked to take part in conferences, to speak, to lecture, to advise. In 1924, for instance, she was deeply involved in an important Conference on Politics, Economics, and Christianity (known as COPEC). The same year she conducted her first Retreat, a new thing for a woman to do in the Church of England. Indeed she did it without any desire to do so—for she was modest and loved quiet work and life. She was constantly breaking new ground. In 1926 for the first time she spoke to the clergy at a small local conference in the Liverpool diocese. She says, "*I* felt funny, but *they* at the beginning more so, and clearly very frightened of me."[18] In the end, however, they became friendly and her addresses* were greatly appreciated, and she was asked to come again. During these later years, too, she was often asked to speak in other churches than her own: to Free Church ministers, and their congregations. She was a little abashed on one occasion by being conducted into the *pulpit* of a Methodist

* Later published as *Concerning the Inner Life.*

church. Behind all this public work—which included lectures to learned societies as well as to religious meetings or conferences—she was writing books, thinking, studying, and doing a great deal of private pastoral work.

PLESHEY AND RETREATS

One aspect of her work after 1924 deserves special mention. In her letters Evelyn Underhill often refers to "my dear Pleshey." Pleshey is a little village in the heart of Essex, several miles out of London, on the Eastern side of the country. It lies among quiet fields and woods and is very old and beautiful with its thatched cottages and its few houses along the village street, an old church, and a few scattered farms. To go there in springtime from the noise of London, was, for a lover of the country, a taste of paradise. To Evelyn Underhill, who greatly preferred the country to the town, it was like "coming home." In springtime the meadows and woods are full of primroses, and a little later the fields are yellow with cowslips. The country is gently undulating, and many of the fields are bordered by trees. The Retreat House stands on the edge of the village. It used to be called "The Holy Land" because there was a Religious House there from the fourteenth century to the Reformation. In 1907, a modern religious community built the present house on the same site, and when they outgrew it and had to move, it was taken over by the diocese of Chelmsford as a Retreat House. A previous warden says of it: "The ground it stands on is holy ground from which prayer has gone up as incense for hundreds of years. Prayer is its life. Its whole atmosphere invites to communion with God."[19]

The Retreat Movement is an integral element in the life of the Church of England, though many Anglicans do not take part in it. More and more people, however, are learning the value of Retreat. Those who were privileged to do this under Evelyn Underhill's guidance were extremely fortunate. Every Retreat begins with a preparatory address, because there are always some people present for the first time; and it is necessary to make it quite clear from the very start what a Retreat should be.

In one of these addresses Evelyn Underhill says:[20]

> *We all know pretty well why we come into Retreat: we come to seek the opportunity of being alone with God and attending to God, in order that we may do His will better in our everyday lives. . . . We do not*

> *come for spiritual information, but for spiritual food and air—to wait on the Lord and renew our strength—not for our own sakes but for the sake of the world.*

Then she goes on to explain what this means, and uses the words of our Lord:[21]

> "SHUT THE DOOR." . . . SHUT *the door. It is an extraordinarily difficult thing to do. . . . It is no use at all to enter that closet, that inner sanctuary, clutching the daily paper, . . . your engagement book and a large bundle of personal correspondence. All these must be left outside. The motto for your Retreat is* GOD ONLY.

The spirit in which she advised her hearers to make the Retreat was one of great simplicity. She often placed some striking quotations in the porch, or some other focus for the thoughts and prayers of those present. On one occasion she pinned up a water-color picture of "St. Francis at Prayer" which a friend had sent her. On another occasion she pinned up some extracts from a French writer, the Abbé de Tourville, about how to behave in Retreat. He says: "Avoid all strain and effort, try to be quiet and passive. . . . Breathe in the grace of God as we breathe in the air. . . . By this deliberate calm and quietude . . . you will gain more than you can conceive."[22] Then he points out that the result of such a Retreat will not be so much *felt*, as that it will almost unconsciously help those who take this line to throw themselves more utterly into the arms of God, sure of his love which is a "fathomless ocean."[23]

All kinds of people came to her Retreats: young and old, men and women. About one such gathering, a first retreatant told her that when she confessed to her husband what she intended to do, he took his pipe from his mouth and said earnestly: "Go, my dear. Go, by all means! You're just about due for a spot of rebirth."[24] Evelyn thought that young husband had certainly hit the nail on the head, for that exactly expresses the reason for Retreat.

At Pleshey, under Evelyn Underhill, the Retreats always followed the same pattern. The Chaplain would celebrate the service of Holy Communion each morning before breakfast; the rest of the day was taken by the Conductor. For a week-end Retreat, the people would gather, if possible, in time for tea on the Friday afternoon; then there would be a hymn practice and a little friendly talk together with perhaps a stroll round the garden and a look at the books in the library. Evensong was at 6:30

and after that silence was kept until after breakfast on the Monday morning. For most people this entering into the silence was like coming home. On the Friday evening Evelyn gave an introductory address; and Saturday and Sunday followed the same pattern: three addresses during the day, a short time of corporate devotion in the chapel at 12:30, a long, free afternoon for rest and exercise, and the day closed with Compline about 9:00 P.M. Between the addresses in the morning and after tea the Conductor was free for interviews, and people were then able to see her about various personal questions.

The atmosphere of these Retreats at Pleshey was very restful and cheerful. Each address was preceded by a session of worship in which the voices rose with such joy that the whole chapel was filled with the spirit of praise. During her addresses Evelyn would often illustrate a point with a witty remark or a funny story, and there would be a burst of delighted laughter. To many of those who were privileged to share in these occasions the lessons learned were beyond words; never could there have been anyone more fitted for this work. The deep and abiding influence of these days of quietness and prayer can never be forgotten.

PASTORAL WORK— SPIRITUAL DIRECTION

If there is one sphere above all others in which Evelyn Underhill excelled, it was in her relations with people on the pastoral side—in what is sometimes called "spiritual direction." For this she had all the necessary gifts of mind and heart. Especially was she able to help the groping intellectual or the rather reluctant agnostic to find firm ground in the Christian faith. This gift revealed itself very early, long before she had herself reached the fullness of faith which came to her later. From her *Letters* we see she began this ministry, though rather diffidently, as early as 1904. In 1907 the same person who had first asked her guidance wrote again, and a long correspondence followed, in which Evelyn Underhill dealt with various difficulties out of her own experience. She ends by saying:[25]

> *You may also take it for granted, of course, that so long as you want the peace and illumination for your own sake, you will not get them. Self-surrender, an entire willingness to live in the dark, in pain, anything —this is the real secret. I think no one really finds the Great Companion till their love is*

of that kind that they long only to GIVE *and not to get.*

All through her life people came to her bringing their troubles and difficulties, many of them seeking faith for the first time. Some came out of complete unbelief, others out of nominal Christianity. To her they owed everything.

One young woman who went to her during those years says that she can never forget the way Evelyn *listened.* It was a winter afternoon; gradually the daylight faded, and still the two sat on in the light of the fire; the house was absolutely quiet, and Evelyn listened, as this girl had never been listened to before; there was a sense of being utterly understood. When Evelyn spoke, at the end, her few words were wise and quiet, and she followed the talk with a letter of direction which was invaluable in its wisdom and loving understanding. Countless people who consulted her must have had a similar experience. And she continued her spiritual direction even when she had barely recovered from one of her frequent illnesses,* or worse still, when she was herself struggling with all kinds of doubts and difficulties, and "nothing seemed real."

* She was subject to constant attacks of asthma, bronchitis, influenza, and similar ills.

Many of her letters are written to people who were overtired or overwrought; to them she gives most sensible advice, telling them to go to bed with a novel and not to overstrain themselves till they feel better. She was herself vehement in temperament so she understood others who were high-strung. She had learned self-control, the use of common sense and humor, and the wise balance between body and soul.

In the published *Letters* she deals with various points which are of value for us all. If she thought her friend was in danger of being too individualistic, she would remind her that some amount of church-going, and above all some sacramental practice, is necessary for us all, for Christianity is a corporate religion. To people in "darkness" and "aridity" she advised regular worship at least once a week if possible at the Eucharist, and a gentle patience with oneself, no overstrain in thought and prayer, and the cultivation of what she called "non-religious interests" such as needlework, drawing, and painting, or music. I am sure she would have added—if she had understood it—cooking and other ordinary and necessary activities.

To all she recommended the making and keeping of a simple Rule of Life:[26]

You will find regular training a great help too. A simple rule, to be followed whether one is in the light or not, gives backbone to one's spiritual life, as nothing else can. You should fix it now, during this time of peace and joy; and let it be decidedly less than you feel you can do now. . . . If you fall later into a state in which you cannot, without strain, practise meditation or mental prayer, you can spend the time in spiritual reading, only try always to keep it [THE SPECIAL TIME] *intact and not use it for other things.*

PERSONAL CHARACTERISTICS

What was Evelyn Underhill like in her later years? She was naturally pale and slight; a woman of middle height. On the street, I imagine, no one would have noticed her particularly for she was the kind of person who does not "light up" until in contact with people. When she did light up—as she always did in any conversation or address—then her face was aglow with intelligence and humor, and often with sweetness and affection. She was a good and witty talker, and a deeply sympathetic person. Before she became a public character, she dressed in a rather out-of-the-world style—not ugly, but peculiar, and a little old-fashioned. But a year or two later all that was changed: she had her hair cut short; she wore charming clothes, in which blue and gray predominated. She was up-to-date, with a difference. She enjoyed social occasions and was welcome in many different circles. Her home was delightful, furnished with taste but without luxury or show. She loved flowers and all growing things and made a country garden out of the London strip at the back of the house. She was very fond of wild flowers, snowdrops perhaps first of all, and then primroses. She was very hospitable and a party at her house was a delightful event for all her guests.

She was also very fond of animals, especially cats. Her letters are full of references to them and are often very amusing.

Although her life was lived practically entirely in London, her real preferences were for the country, whether the quiet scenery of southern England or the Scottish hills or the mountains of Switzerland. She was not strong enough for actual climbing, but whenever she was in mountain country she always wanted to get as high as possible and to the most solitary places with vast views. In her Retreat addresses she would often speak of the mountains, saying that to come apart like this for a short time ought to be a "mountain" experience. In one place she writes:[27]

> *I remember once in the Alps finding myself alone in a high pasture surrounded by the strange almost unearthly mountain life. I was filled then with that absolute contentment and solemn happiness which hardly anything else can give to those who have the mountain sense.*

And in a Retreat she urged her hearers to

> *look across the valley and see the great spiritual snowfields in their beauty.*

Such a love of mountains inevitably makes us think of One who rose early to pray and spent many a night alone on a mountain top—alone with God.

Evelyn Underhill was a balanced person. She knew that most of us cannot remain on the mountain, we have to come down to the plain. She lived the greater part of her life in the heart of a great city, accepting fully all the claims of family and friendship and of hard work in her vocation and ministry. She had a full share of suffering, though she would never have called it that: in her later years her health was never very good and all she did was at great cost to herself. She knew the deep trial of inward darkness and spiritual suffering when God seemed far away and there was no light.

What she taught, she lived. In one place she sums this up—unconsciously—in these words:[28]

> *Pure Love or Charity—utter self-giving which is our reply to the Love of God—is the same as sanctity. What is pure love? That which gives and gives and never demands. In the words of Gertrude More:* COURAGEOUS, HUMBLE, CONSTANT: NOT WORN OUT WITH LABOURS, NOT DAUNTED BY DIFFICULTIES—*bravely sticking it out when tired, disheartened, worried. And to do this, we look beyond it all, trying to respond to the Love of God, seeking and serving Christ in our fellow-men. If we do that faithfully, give ourselves to God's purposes, we will develop such depth of peaceful, devoted love as passes beyond the need of being fed by feeling or the consolations of religion. . . . Do not make the mistake of thinking if you feel cold and dead, that you do not know how to love.*

Beyond her learning and her books, beyond all her efforts to serve and help others, what was her special contribution to the world which she still blesses by her influence? Charles Williams says: "Her vocation was rather to be—a guide? no; say rather, in the end, a light. The light might, and certainly did, illuminate and guide, but first it merely shone"[29]—and even when she did not know it. A friend visited her one day in her London home. Evelyn had just been very ill. "The door of the room into which I was shown was directly behind the big armchair in which she was sitting facing a glowing fire. As I entered she got up and turned round, looking so fragile as though 'a puff of wind might blow her away' might be literally true in her case, *but* light simply streamed from her face illuminated with a radiant smile." This friend says that she never saw this again, but that this sight told her "more of God and of the Mystical Body than all her work put together."[30]

Such a glimpse of the "glory of God" in a human being is rare, but it has been seen elsewhere, now and again, in special persons. Usually all that *we* see in a saint—at close quarters—is an unobtrusive person who does "everything that any other decent person does only somewhat better and with a totally different point of view." Bishop Lumsden

Barkway, speaking of Evelyn, says very aptly: "Her holiness was of the type which hid itself in the apparent 'ordinariness' of her outward life."[31]

LATER YEARS

As we study the record of Evelyn's later years we realize that it was then that her most important work was done. To herself, possibly, the work of giving Retreats was the most worthwhile thing she ever did. It was that and her unofficial pastoral ministry which meant most to her. But all through these years her work as a writer went on. The contrast between her book on *Mysticism* and her great book on *Worship* (published in 1936) shows how far she had traveled along the way of Christian faith and practice in the interval. It was during these years that she became more and more a humble practicing member of the Anglican Church, quite content to be where God had placed her. She did this without any loss of charity or of breadth of outlook, and with an increasing desire for Christian unity.

During this final period her health became more uncertain till at last she was compelled to give up all public speaking and retreats. When war broke out in 1939 she came out decidedly as a Christian

House of Retreat
Pleshey, Chelmsford, England

pacifist. But now most of her outward work was done. She and her husband went into the country, where for a short time she helped in parish work until she was laid low by a very severe illness. In 1940 they went back to London, living with friends on the heights of Hampstead, surrounded by the noise of air-raids and alarms—all of which she took very calmly. When she was well enough she wrote a little, including a quarterly letter to a prayer group which had asked for her help a short time before. She was at peace, though often in much physical weakness. In the spring of 1941 she seemed much better, and she began to move about more freely. Suddenly, without warning, she died, on Sunday, June 15, 1941. But though she passed in silence, surely it was true of her, as of Gore* when he lay dying, that behind the veil of consciousness there was the dawning of delight. "Transcendent Glory, transcendent Glory," murmured Gore; and Evelyn Underhill knew, too, that[32]

Glory is the final word of religion,
as joy is its final state.

* Charles Gore (1853-1932), English bishop, and author of many religious works, who sought to reconcile the Christian creed with the growth of scientific, historic, and critical knowledge.

In the Chapel at Pleshey there is a memorial to Evelyn Underhill. At the service at which it was dedicated this prayer was offered:

O God, who by the lives of those who love
Thee dost refashion the souls of men,
We give thanks for the ministry of Thy
servant Evelyn:
In whose life and words Thy love and
majesty were made known to us,
Whose loving spirit set our spirits on fire,
Who learnt from Thee the Shepherd's care
for his sheep:
Grant that some measure of the Spirit
Which she received from Thee may fall on
us who love her.
We ask it for the sake of Jesus Christ our
Lord. AMEN.

*EVELYN UNDERHILL'S THE SPIRITUAL LIFE**

IN THESE FOUR BROADCASTS upon the spiritual life, Evelyn Underhill gives us a summary of *the main points of her teaching on this subject*. Of all her books this is the smallest, but it is packed with thought and experience. Almost every sentence could be expanded into a chapter. Of course it does not cover all the aspects of her message, but it does gather up much of her thought on one vital aspect of her teaching. Behind it there lies a wealth of study, insight, and experience (pp. 30-31).

> *The first question here is not "What is best for my soul?" nor is it even "What is most useful to humanity?" But—transcending both these limited aims—what function must this life fulfil in the great and secret economy of God?*

* Quotations from *The Spiritual Life* by Evelyn Underhill are identified by the page number on which they appear. They are reprinted from the Harper & Row edition, and used by permission of Hodder & Stoughton, Ltd., London.

. . . dealing with ourselves
and attending to God . . .

WHAT IS THE SPIRITUAL LIFE?
[PART I]

In Part I she explains what she means by "the spiritual life." The definition she gives is the key-note of this chapter (p. 32):

> *A spiritual life is simply a life in which all that we do comes from the centre, where we are anchored in God: a life soaked through and through by a sense of His reality and claim, and self-given to the great movement of His will.*

In her other writings she expands this definition in various ways. First of all, she insists that *this life is open to all.* It is not for a favored few or for people who "are made that way." This is an important point and needs to be grasped from the outset because far too many people are either not interested in the spiritual life and think it is "not for them"; or they think so poorly of themselves that they assume that a spiritual life can only be meant for people with greater opportunities or gifts than they think they possess. From the beginning she wants us to accept the truth that this life is offered to all—without exception—whatever our circumstances. This means that the spiritual life is not another "life" somehow "tacked on" to the ordinary life in which we are all involved (p. 24), but that it is the very meaning of the ordinary common life of mankind.

Secondly, it is a life of trust—of freedom from fear and anxiety. This means that it is a spacious life, because we lose the sense of being imprisoned by circumstances. In her *The House of the Soul*, she gives a beautiful illustration of this trustful spirit in the life of birds. She reminds us that in their carefree lives they show the spirit in which we ought to live, for we are "of more value than many sparrows." She pictures them flying with absolute certainty for thousands of miles through the air, over uncharted seas, sure that there *is* a country which is the haven of their hearts' desire.

The essence of the spiritual life is LOVE; this means being given to God and then to the whole world. On this she quotes a mystic who said: "*God cannot lodge in a narrow heart: our hearts are as great as our love.*" This implies that for each one of us the spiritual life should be always growing *up* and *out*; and we do this as members of the Body of Christ, each with our special job, balancing and completing each other. She adds, in her humorous way: "The body has many members, some of them a very funny shape!"

But we must accept the fact that we are none of us perfect, yet, if we are given to God and to our fellows, God does use us. Again and again, in various ways, she points out that we need the service both of Martha and of Mary.

Another point she makes is that the spiritual life is a *growth* (pp. 26-27). This is another way of speaking of Christian perfection or sanctification—as in the case of our two previous writers, Fénelon and Wesley. This growth is *hidden* from ourselves and usually from other people, though sometimes they may see changes for the better without having any idea of the cause. Even our Lord's life as man was one of growth: his prayers as a child at Nazareth prepared him for his prayers as a man, and finally for the awful prayers of the Passion:[33]

> *Just so the light of the Spirit is to unfold gently and steadily within us, till at last our final stature, all God designed for us, is attained.*

This spiritual growth is due to God's creative action; as we yield to him he works on, and in us, through all the circumstances of our lives. But we cannot see what is going on, and we need great patience with ourselves: "Rest in the LORD and wait patiently for him" (Ps. 37:7). This means being willing to accept suffering, darkness, difficulties of all kinds—when they come. Through all these experiences we have to learn not to say *Mine* but *Ours.*

To learn to live a creative life of this kind evidently means accepting a good deal of discipline. In *The Golden Sequence* she says that[34]

> *this cleansing, bracing and transforming of the will and emotional life is the hardest and most searching of all the soul's purifications. For it requires us to take the Cross into the most hidden sanctuary of personality.*

We have to be willing to be purged from self-love in every nook and cranny of our hearts. This reminds us of the stern words of Fénelon about the absolute necessity of death to self if we are to live unto God.

In the same book Evelyn Underhill likens the discipline of the spiritual life to the experience of the mountaineer[35] who has to undergo a severe training beginning with smaller climbs till he can do more and meet sterner challenges. The spiritual traveler has to be willing to climb along a narrow path, to be watchful at every moment, never to look down at the depths beneath, but to follow his guide without flinching and to keep on the track even when he can't see a step ahead and has no idea where the guide is leading him. In the spiritual life we have to learn to renounce all self-pity, all desire to be treated leniently. We are out on the finest climb of all: the ascent of the spirit. Only then can God use us for the more difficult tasks of his kingdom.

. . . I saw the race fulfil
the spiral of its steep ascent,
predestined of the Will . . .

. . . *"Here am I! Send me!"* . . .

THE SPIRITUAL LIFE
AS COMMUNION WITH GOD
. . . AS CO-OPERATION WITH GOD
[PARTS II AND III]

These two sections hang together. They deal exclusively with the subject of prayer. In one of her addresses to clergy Evelyn Underhill says very clearly that[36]

> *A real man of prayer . . . is one who deliberately wills and steadily desires that his intercourse with God and other souls shall be controlled and actuated at every point by God Himself.*

She says that such a person does not necessarily "say" a great many prayers, or even offer an enormous number of definite intercessions for people or causes; such practices depend more upon a particular temperament and vocation. But a real man of prayer is a person who is deeply attached to God in heart and will and—as far as he possibly can be—is given up to God, to be led by him both in his prayer and in his work. What she says here she means not only for the clergy, to whom she was then speaking, but for every Christian man and woman. *All* are called to live like this; for this is the *normal* Christian life, the life implied as the will of God for us all in the New Testament (p. 45). After all, when our Lord spoke of prayer and of loving God with all our hearts, he was talking to people like ourselves with just the same temptations and worries and difficulties, and he takes for granted that we shall turn to God in all simplicity and want to be and to do what he wills. As she says in this little book, the Lord's Prayer sums it all up and shows us more plainly than anything else the way in which we are meant to pray and to live: wholly for God and his kingdom (p. 77).

> *I go back to the one perfect summary of man's Godward life and call—the Lord's Prayer. Consider how dynamic and purposive is its character. Thy Will be* DONE—*Thy Kingdom* COME*! There is energy, drive, purpose in those words; an intensity*

of desire for the coming of perfection into life. Not the limp resignation . . . but a total concentration on the total interests of God, which must be expressed in action.

In her great book on *Worship* she deals fully with the importance of personal worship within the framework of the whole life of the church. As she puts it:[37]

The "praying Church"
is built of praying souls.

And the quality of the life of the church as a whole depends upon the depth and reality of the prayer of each member. For even great religious awakenings have been due (though often this is not realized) to the hidden prayer of deep dedication of some unknown, obscure individual. And this hidden life goes on all the time, carried forward from one generation to another by all who enter into this stream of prayer and worship which is the very life of the church universal.

Here, as in all her books, her teaching on prayer is based upon a definite pattern. She ascribes this particular pattern to Bérulle; but the pattern itself, though expressed in other words, is very ancient, going back to the days of the Early Church; St.

Ambrose* called it *The Three Seals.* As she says (pp. 58-59), "One of the great French teachers of the seventeenth century, Cardinal de Bérulle, summed up the relation of man to God in three words":

Adoration—Adherence—Co-operation

Sometimes she makes this clearer by a change of wording:

Adoration—Communion—Action

It is a most satisfying pattern. The more we try to use it the more we find it fits into every situation. For instance, if we examine the teachings of St. Paul on prayer (as we can glean them from scattered references in his letters)†, we find that his emphasis is on the same lines. If we go back, above all, to the gospel and study the Lord's Prayer, and John 17, we find the same pattern: *God first*, and all the time; then our offering of ourselves to him for his use and his kingdom; and finally, prayer for the whole of mankind in its sins and temptations. The whole is

* St. Ambrose (c. 339-397), Bishop of Milan.

† See *Paul, Man of Prayer,* a leaflet by Maud H. Lynch. Order from Literature Headquarters, 7820 Reading Road, Cincinnati 37, Ohio. Single copies free; 25 copies, 20 cents.

gathered up once more in an act of loving and adoring worship. For personal worship means that we answer the gift of the love of God with the loving gift of ourselves. As she puts it: there are (p. 59)

> *three kinds of generosity . . .*
> *three kinds of self-forgetfulness*
> *. . . the formula of the spiritual life.*

But when we try to practice this kind of prayer, we may find it very difficult. For many of us it seems the very opposite of what we want to do. Instinctively we want to begin by speaking to God about *ourselves*, our difficulties and needs, and only later on—"if we have time" or inclination—do we think of praising and adoring him. In many Christian circles adoration is either not understood at all, or is only practiced fitfully, when we "feel moved" to do it. Now, of course, it is perfectly true that Jesus taught us to "bring everything to the Lord in prayer." The petition for daily bread in the Lord's Prayer covers everything we can possibly want to say, in the simplest and most trustful way. But we notice that this petition comes *after* we have prayed that God's name may be hallowed, his kingdom come, his will be done. It is in *that* setting that Christ teaches us to bring all our necessities and desires to God, in order that we may be able to live in obedience to his will and be used in the work of his kingdom.

Now let us think more fully about these three points.

ADORATION. "Adoration is . . . the seed from which all other prayer must spring."[38] This implies the fact of conversion: the moment, whether it comes suddenly or gradually, when the reality of God seizes hold of us, and we *know* that he is the only Reality, that he alone matters. Still more epoch-making is the moment when we realize that this Holy God is Love, and that *he loves us*. This reminds us of the Scottish scholar who had been tortured with doubts and temptations; he said: "When I knew that God loved me, I danced on the Brig' o' Dee with delight!"[39]

In all her writings Evelyn Underhill reiterates that adoration is delight in God *for Himself*, joy that He is God: in whom all Beauty and Goodness have their source, whose will is good beyond our imagining, whose service is perfect freedom. Adoration, however, transcends thought and feeling. Sometimes it may be accompanied by a solemn joy; but the deepest adoration may be offered in those moments of blankness or desolation when all we can do is to offer ourselves to God as we are, and then try to do our work in the sure faith that he has accepted our offering, though we can *feel* no difference. For the essence of adoration is self-offering; and it is only real when it includes everything: our life, our work, ourselves.

In her beautiful book, *The Golden Sequence*, Evelyn Underhill points out that[40]

> *. . . when we come to the practice of this surrendered adoration, so difficult to the troubled and arrogant soul of the modern world,*

there is not nearly so much difference as we should expect between our own efforts of worship and those of primitive man: for "the world's altar-stairs begin in the jungle."[40] A friend of mine who lived in Central Africa many years ago often used to speak of the emotion aroused in her when, at some exquisitely lovely spot in the forest, she would find under a tree or by a waterfall, a little "spirit hut" with a few flowers or some other humble offering to the spirit of beauty, which the African pagan laid there in token of his worship.

On the island of Iona off the west coast of Scotland in the summer months when a conference or camp is being held, very often the members make a pilgrimage round the island, stopping at all the points connected with the life of St. Columba.* There, under the sky and in view of the Atlantic, they sing and pray, praising God for his beauty in Creation and for his love to the world proclaimed by this great saint and missionary all those centuries ago. To stay in Iona is to feel and know the power of prayer, for every stone and rock seems impregnated with the presence of God. Adoration unites us with the whole church of God down the ages and with the whole family of mankind.

COMMUNION OR ADHERENCE. In *adoration* we are drawn to worship by the wonder and glory of the greatness of God, the Father Almighty. The classic passage for our meditation on this subject is the story of the vision and call of the prophet Isaiah in Isaiah 6.

But God is not only infinitely above and beyond us, he is also infinitely near: "Peace to him that is far off, and to him that is near" (Isa. 57:19). Even in the Old Testament men knew this: "Thou hast beset me behind and before, and laid thine hand upon me" (Ps. 139:5), says the Psalmist in wonder and

* St. Columba, Irish missionary, called "Apostle of Caledonia," who established the monastery on the island of Iona in A.D. 563 and converted the northern Picts of Scotland. Today the monastery, rebuilt by Protestant ministers and laymen, is a center for retreats and Christian renewal.

delight. Still more do we know Him *near* in Jesus Christ our Lord. The Gospel of Matthew begins with the thought of him as *Emmanuel* (God with us), and ends with the promise: "Lo, I am with you alway, even unto the end of the world" (Matt. 28: 20). So the prayer of communion includes every kind of prayer in which, by faith, we know that Christ is very near. Sometimes we feel it. At others we *know* that he is near simply by faith; we have his word for it, and that is enough. *He is with us, and will never leave us;* and he wants us to turn to him at all times and in all circumstances. He will never let us down.

This prayer of communion can be practiced in different ways: sometimes we may take a passage from the Gospels and think about it. Above all, we try to *look* at Jesus in it and watch the way he behaves to people, and the way he speaks to us now. Then, at once, by an act of faith we open our hearts to him and pray to him as a "man speaks to his friend." At other times we may feel led to "wait upon God" quietly, almost in silence. Here our attitude should be childlike in its simplicity. A small boy once went to see a woman who always gave him flowers when she came back from the country; he had taken his flowers and had run downstairs with them. A few minutes later he came back again: "What do you want now, Johnny?" said his friend. He looked at her and said simply: "I don't want anything . . . I only want to be with you." No prayer could be more pleasing to our Lord than simply to "want to be with him." Sometimes this kind of prayer is "given" to us in the form of a great quietness—something we could never reach by any effort of our own. When this is given, we should wait thankfully and quietly until it seems time to move. Then make a deliberate act of self-offering to Christ and go on to the next duty or trial in his peace and power. Out of such prayer comes a sense of being guided and supported by God in all kinds of ways:[41]

> *Opening paths, suggesting sacrifices, bringing about those unforeseen events and relationships which condition the soul's advance.*

CO-OPERATION. Evelyn Underhill explains this very clearly in our book (p. 75):

> *He [God] made us in order to use us, and use us in the most profitable way; for His purpose, not ours. To live a spiritual life means subordinating all other interests to that single fact.*

This co-operation with God for his purpose is achieved in three different ways: (a) by giving ourselves to God in order to be ourselves transformed and made fit to be tools of his ceaseless work of love; (b) through prayer of all kinds, but particularly through intercessions; (c) through service, work, effort, and toil, and through suffering. Such co-operation is costly.

In *The Golden Sequence* Evelyn Underhill speaks of this third way of the spiritual life as "action" rather than "co-operation" though she means the same thing. Here she points out that God has made us for himself[42]

not only to be worshippers,
but to be workmen.

That is why we have to undergo all kinds of discipline if we are to be trained as his messengers or his instruments. Intercession is then seen to be not a forcing of our needs upon God—as though he needed to be reminded—but as[43]

part of the creative action of God.

We do not originate our prayer; it is inspired by God himself. He then takes our willing self-offering, and in some mysterious way uses it for the blessing and healing of people in every kind of need. "His Spirit within us is actually praying for us,"[44] says St. Paul. God is working for our good all the time; when we offer ourselves to him, he accepts and uses our prayers in ways beyond our understanding, though now and then we may see results. In the same chapter she says that, in this co-operation with God,[45]

> *Here we are surely face to face with one of the great mysteries of that spiritual world in which our real lives are lived. . . . We cannot understand it, but perhaps we grasp its reality better if we keep in mind two facts. The first is, that all experience proves that we are not separate, ring-fenced spirits.*
>
> *We penetrate each other, influence each other for good or evil . . . all the time. . . . We are all linked in Him. Therefore it is literally true that the secret pressure of the Eternal is present in all movements of mutual service and love.*

Since we are so linked, we are all needed for the whole; not one of us is useless.

We are woven together, the bright threads and the dull, to form a living tissue . . .

Thus effective intercession depends both upon keeping our hearts open to God in love and obedience and on keeping on the alert to all the needs of the world, ready to pray and serve and love in any way that seems possible in our circumstances.[46]

Only a charity poured out in both directions can become and remain a channel of the Spirit's Will.

Inevitably this will mean a good deal of suffering; this can, and should, be offered for the healing of the wounds of the world, in union with the ever-living intercession of Christ, our Great High Priest.

. . . . to live more and more towards Him only . . .

. . . the constant offering
of our wills to God . . .

SOME QUESTIONS AND DIFFICULTIES
[PART IV]

HOW DO WE EXPLAIN SUFFERING AND EVIL? In a short talk like this obviously Evelyn Underhill could not do more than touch on this crucial question. But in her *Letters* to individuals and in her books she speaks frequently of suffering. She never attempts to explain it, but accepts it as a fact which is part of the spiritual life as well as of the ordinary life of mankind. To her it was not a "problem," but a "mystery." But her sense of the greatness, the holiness, and the love of God was so strong that she could accept where she could not understand. In a letter to C. S. Lewis she thanks him for his book, *The Problem of Pain.* She tells him she has thought a great deal about the subject of pain and evil, and that she is extremely grateful to him for the way in which he has[47]

> *. . . related the fact of suffering to the eternal background of our life.*
>
> *Myself, I cannot get much beyond von Hügel's conclusion, that Christianity does not explain suffering but does show us what to do with it.*

In her *Letters* and other writings she constantly alludes to the value of suffering when endured and offered to God as "sacrifice." In one of her retreat addresses on *The Cross and the Sacraments* she related the whole problem of suffering to the cross:[48]

> *Our world is chaos without the Cross; for we never understand suffering until we have embraced it, turned it into sacrifice and given ourselves in it to God.*

Then she makes the piercing remark:[49]

> *We often think we need a quiet time before we make a great spiritual effort. Christ's quiet time was Gethsemane, and we know what that was like.*

She reminds us that every time we go to Communion we go to receive the very mind and spirit of him who gave himself for us on the cross. Suffering comes to us all. It is the way we take it that transforms it from a burden into a willing sacrifice which God can use. She says:[50]*

There is always a night-shift and
sooner or later we are put on it.

When these trials come we should accept them in the spirit of the Psalmist: "Ye servants of the LORD, which by night stand in the house of the LORD. Lift up your hands in the sanctuary, and bless the LORD" (Ps. 134:2-3). Then she turns to some practical difficulties.

HOW CAN WE FIND AND DO THE WILL OF GOD? She suggests that there are two ways of finding out: one is by looking at our whole practical problem in the light of the general teaching of Christ and the main truths and principles of the Christian faith. Sometimes this will be enough to give us the light we need, for God has made his general will quite plain in the Bible. And if we do not know our Bible very well, now is the time to get some help in studying it for ourselves.

But we may be quite clear on this main point, and yet not know which of two equally good things we

* Also see *Dimensions of Prayer* by Douglas V. Steere, p. 110. (Literature Headquarters, 7820 Reading Road, Cincinnati 37, Ohio, $1.00.)

ought to choose. Then we should resort to prayer, but prayer of a certain kind: not the urgent excited petition of someone who wants his own way and is afraid he will not get it; but rather in the quiet spirit of surrender, of "waiting on God" until we are quiet enough to be able to give up our own preferences, our likes and dislikes, and look at the matter quite objectively, only wanting the will of God to be done.

This may take some time, but, when we are in this spirit of obedience, then we can look quite calmly at both sides of the question and ask ourselves: to which side do I seem to be drawn? Once the decision is made in this spirit we should never go back on it but go forward, believing that the whole matter is now in the hands of God and that he can make it all come right, even if we may feel—at times—that we have been mistaken.

ARE OUR "SPIRITUAL EXPERIENCES" MERELY DISGUISED WISH-FULFILMENT? On this she says two things (pp. 115-116):

> *In the first place, the complete expression of everything of which we are capable—the whole psychological zoo living within us, as well as the embryonic beginnings of artist, statesman or saint—means chaos, not character.*

As to the attempt to discredit the spiritual life as a form of wish-fulfilment, this has to meet the plain fact that the real life of the Spirit has little to do with emotional enjoyments, even of the loftiest kind. Indeed, it offers few attractions to the natural man; nor does it set out to satisfy his personal desires.

Here she implies that the very question shows a complete misunderstanding of the nature of the spiritual life itself; hence it is an unreal question.

Then she deals with a question which is always relevant and affects us all nowadays just as much as when she was giving these talks: the question of lack of time and privacy for prayer. She was well aware that this was—as it is now—a very real problem for great numbers of people who long to lead a spiritual life and yet feel that circumstances are against them. Very wisely she points out that it is not so much the amount of *time* that matters as the spirit in which we live. The *constant* offering of our wills to God throughout the day with little darts of prayer is what she recommends. She understood the rush of modern life, and she knew that many of the people who came to her could rarely get the quiet they needed, either because of long hours of work, or because of the unending pressure of home duties. She used to say to them all that "some time, even though this may be a very short time, [should be regularly] given and given definitely to communion with Him [for prayer and thought]" (p. 120).

In her *Letters* she gives advice suitable to the persons to whom she is writing. She never pitched it too high for people who could not keep it up. But she would remind them that our Lord spoke of prayer as the most natural thing in the world to people whose lives were as crowded with work and worries as are our lives today and, to add to that, most of the people to whom he spoke were already enduring the pressure of foreign occupation. In all circumstances we *can* pray because we have been made for God and, therefore, for prayer.

All the teachings in this little book are the distilled essence of a living experience. As we read and try to learn from Evelyn Underhill, we should remind ourselves frequently that, although she was so far above and beyond us in so many ways, she was also very natural, gay, and humble. She could worship anywhere, and with gladness, for her heart was at rest. See how naturally she speaks of worshiping in the little church of San Damiano at Assisi, where "the lay congregation consisted of half a dozen peasants, a few mosquitoes, and myself." In one of her poems she speaks for us all when she pictures us[51]

. . . groping dull and blind
Within the sheltering dimness of thy wings
. . .

and then:

We, out of age-long wandering, but come
Back to our Father's heart,
Where now we are at home.

NOTES

FOREWORD

1. William E. Sangster, *The Pure in Heart* (New York: Abingdon Press, 1954), p. 250.

FRANÇOIS FÉNELON AND CHRISTIAN PERFECTION

1. Ély Carcassonne, *Fénelon: L'Homme et L'Oeuvre* (Paris: Hatier-Boivin, 1946), p. 6.
2. Victor Duruy, *A Short History of France*, trans. by L. C. Jane and Lucy Menzies (New York: E. P. Dutton & Co., Inc., n.d.) Everyman's Library, Vol. II, pp. 133-134.
3. Duruy, Vol. II, p. 1.
4. Carcassonne, p. 8.
5. Carcassonne, p. 12.
6. Carcassonne, p. 29.
7. Attributed to New York message in *The Times* (London), dated February 9, 1933, by Ronald Knox, *Enthusiasm* (New York: Oxford University Press, 1950), p. 582.
8. See François Varillon, *Fénelon et le Pur Amour* from the collection *Maîtres Spirituels* (Paris: Edition du Seuil, 1957), p. 6, and Carcassonne, p. 71.
9. Carcassonne, p. 142.
10. Extract from Agnès de La Gorce, *Le Vrai Visage*

de *Fénelon* from the collection *Bibliothèque Variea* (Paris: Librairie Hachette, Editeur, 1958), p. 249.

11. *Oeuvres Spirituelles de Fénelon* (Paris, 1802) 4 vol., Vol. IV, pp. 379-381. Translated by Olive Wyon.
12. Carcassonne, p. 154.
13. Varillon, p. 113.
14. Gerald Vann, *The Heart of Man* (New York: Longmans, Green & Co., Inc., 1945), p. 61. By courtesy of Geoffrey Bless, Ltd., London.
15. Varillon, p. 119.
16. Caryll Houselander, *Guilt* (New York: Sheed & Ward, 1951), p. 29.
17. Duruy, p. 203.

JOHN WESLEY AND CHRISTIAN PERFECTION

1. John Wesley, *The Journal of the Rev. John Wesley, A.M.*, ed. by Nehemiah Curnock (New York: Eaton & Mains, 1909-1916), 8 vol., Vol. III, pp. 13-15, May 30, 1742.
2. Quoted by John Telford in his *The Life of John Wesley* (New York: Hunt & Eaton, n.d.), p. 19. Permission granted by Epworth Press, London, and Alec R. Allenson, agent, Naperville, Ill.
3. Quoted by Telford, pp. 19-20.
4. Wesley, *Journal*, Vol. I, pp. 470-472, May 24, 1738.

5. Telford, p. 93.
6. Wesley, *Journal*, Vol. I, p. 442, March 4, 1738.
7. Wesley, *Journal*, Vol. I, p. 472, May 24, 1738.
8. Wesley, *Journal*, Vol I, p. 476, May 24 and 25, 1738.
9. Wesley, *Journal*, Vol. II, p. 156, March 10, 1739.
10. Wesley, *Journal*, Vol. II, p. 167, March 29, 1739.
11. Wesley, *Journal*, Vol. II, pp. 172-173, April 2, 1739.
12. John R. Green, *Short History of the English People* (New York: E. P. Dutton & Co., Everyman's Library, rev. 1952), Vol. II.
13. Robert F. Wearmouth, *Methodism and the Common People in the 18th Century* (London: Epworth Press, 1945), p. 77.
14. Wesley, *Journal*, Vol. II, pp. 220, 223, 273. June 14, 1739; June 17, 1739; Sept. 9, 1739.
15. Wesley, *Journal*, abridged and ed. by Percy Livingstone Parker, appreciation by Augustine Birrell, and introduction by Hugh Price Hughes (London: Sir Isaac Pittman & Sons, 1902), p. 479, August 18, 1789. Used by permission of Moody Press, Chicago.
16. W. H. Hutton, *John Wesley* (London: The Macmillan Co., Ltd., 1927), p. vii.
17. G. H. Trevelyan, *English Social History* (3rd ed.; New York: Longmans, Green & Co.,

1946), p. 362. Courtesy of David McKay Co., Inc.

18. Wesley, *Journal*, Vol. VII, pp. 42-43, January 4, 1785.
19. See John Alfred Faulkner, *Wesley as Sociologist, Theologian, Churchman* (New York: Methodist Book Concern, 1918), pp. 27-28.
20. John Wesley, *Letters of the Rev. John Wesley, A.M.*, ed. by John Telford (London: Epworth Press, 1931), Vol. VIII, p. 265, February 24, 1791.
21. Quoted by Faulkner, pp. 19-21.
22. See Wesley, *Journal*, Vol. VIII, p. 35, January 1, 1790.
23. Telford, pp. 350-351.
24. Quoted by Telford, "Introduction," p. xii, from William Edward Hartpole Lecky, *A History of England in the XVIIIth Century* (New York: D. Appleton & Co., 1878), 8 vol., Vol. II, p. 567.
25. Green, p. 696.
26. John M. Todd, *John Wesley and the Catholic Church* (New York: The Macmillan Co., 1959), p. 192.
27. Maximin Piette, *John Wesley in the Evolution of Protestantism* (Paris: Picard et Fils, 1927), limited ed.
28. Henry Bett, *The Spirit of Methodism* (Nashville: M.E. Church, South, 1911), p. 10.

29. William E. Sangster, *The Path to Perfec An Examination and Restatement of Wesley's Doctrine of Christian Perfe* (New York: Abingdon-Cokesbury, 19 p. 98. Published 1961 by Epworth I London; Alec R. Allenson, Naperville, U.S.A., distributors.
30. Sangster, *The Path to Perfection*, p. 103.
31. Robert Newton Flew, *Idea of Perfectio Christian Theology* (London: Oxford versity Press, 1934), pp. 324-328.
32. Wesley, *Letters*, Vol. IV, p. 213 (to Mrs. M land), May 26, 1763.
33. *The Methodist Hymnal* (New York: Meth Book Concern, 1939), No. 344.
34. St. Francis de Sales, *Introduction to the De Life*, trans. and ed. by John K. Ryan introduction by Douglas V. Steere (N York: Harper & Row, Publishers, Inc., 19 52), p. xxx.
35. See Sangster, *The Pure in Heart*, p. 187.
36. Sangster, *The Pure in Heart*, p. 234.
37. Sangster, *The Pure in Heart*, p. 188.
38. See Sangster, *The Pure in Heart*, pp. 170-1 and Wesley, *Journal*, December 23, 1744.
39. As quoted by E. B. Chappell, *Studies in the L of John Wesley* (Nashville: Publishing Ho M.E. Church, South, 1915), p. 218.
40. Bett, pp. 37-38.

41. Sangster, *The Pure in Heart*, p. 105.
42. Ronald A. Knox, *Enthusiasm, A Chapter in the History of Religion* (New York: Oxford University Press, © 1950), pp. 125, 136.
43. Ray Strachey, *Group Movements of the Past and Experiments in Guidance* (London: Faber & Faber, Ltd., 1934), pp. 167, 163, 165, 157.
44. Wesley, *Journal*, Vol. V, p. 426, August 12, 1771.
45. Knox, p. 539.
46. Knox, p. 540.
47. Wesley, *Journal*, Vol. V, pp. 324-325, June 27, 1769.
48. Sangster, *The Path to Perfection*, pp. 194-195.
49. Sangster, *The Path to Perfection*, p. 194.
50. Sangster, *The Pure in Heart*, p. 250.

EVELYN UNDERHILL AND THE SPIRITUAL LIFE

1. Evelyn Underhill, *Immanence, A Book of Verses* (New York: E. P. Dutton & Co., Inc., 1912), pp. 13-15.
2. Lucy Menzies, "Memoir," preface to Evelyn Underhill's *Light of Christ* (published in *Light of Christ—The Fruits of the Spirit—Abba*, three books in one volume) (New York: Longmans, Green & Co., Inc., 1956), p. 18. Courtesy of David McKay Co., Inc.
3. Evelyn Underhill, *Abba* (published in *Light of*

Christ—The Fruits of the Spirit—Abba), see above, pp. 85-87.

4. Underhill, *Light of Christ*, "Memoir" by Menzies, p. 18.
5. Evelyn Underhill, *The Letters of Evelyn Underhill*, edited with an "Introduction" by Charles Williams (New York: Longmans, Green & Co., Inc., 1943), p. 8. Courtesy of David McKay Co., Inc.
6. Underhill, *Letters*, "Introduction" by Williams, p. 11.
7. Underhill, *Letters*, "Introduction" by Williams, p. 11.
8. Margaret Cropper, *Life of Evelyn Underhill* (New York: Harper & Row, Inc., 1958), p. 16.
9. Cropper, p. 19.
10. Cropper, p. 18.
11. Cropper, p. 27.
12. Cropper, p. 58.
13. Cropper, p. 65.
14. Underhill, *Letters*, "Introduction" by Williams, p. 13.
15. Underhill, *Letters*, pp. 126-127.
16. Underhill, *Letters*, "Introduction" by Williams, p. 26.
17. Underhill, *Letters*, "Introduction" by Williams, pp. 26-27.
18. Cropper, p. 137.

19. Underhill, *Light of Christ*, "Memoir" by Menzies, p. 12.
20. Underhill, *The Fruits of the Spirit*, p. 1.
21. Underhill, *The Fruits of the Spirit*, pp. 1-2.
22. Underhill, *Light of Christ*, "Memoir" by Menzies, p. 14.
23. Underhill, *Light of Christ*, "Memoir" by Menzies, p. 15.
24. Underhill, *Light of Christ*, "The Need of Retreat," p. 102.
25. Underhill, *Letters*, p. 64.
26. Underhill, *Letters*, p. 312.
27. Underhill, *Light of Christ*, "Memoir" by Menzies, pp. 15-16.
28. Evelyn Underhill, *Anthology of the Love of God*, edited by Bishop Lumsden Barkway and Lucy Menzies (New York: David McKay Co., 1954), pp. 29-30.
29. Underhill, *Letters*, "Introduction" by Williams, p. 44.
30. Underhill, *Letters*, "Introduction" by Williams, p. 37.
31. Underhill, *Anthology of the Love of God*, "Introduction" by Barkway, p. 19.
32. Underhill, *Abba*, p. 85.
33. Underhill, *The Light of Christ*, p. 45.
34. Evelyn Underhill, *The Golden Sequence* (New York: Harper & Row, Inc., 1960), p. 140. Copyright by E. P. Dutton & Co., Inc., 1933.

35. Underhill, *The Golden Sequence*, pp. 104-105.
36. Evelyn Underhill, *Concerning the Inner Life* (New York: E. P. Dutton & Co., Inc., 1926), p. 4.
37. Evelyn Underhill, *Worship* (New York: Harper & Row, Inc., © 1936), p. 163. By permission of James Nisbet & Co., Ltd., London.
38. Underhill, *The Golden Sequence*, p. 162.
39. Underhill, *The Anthology of the Love of God*, "Introduction" by Barkway, pp. 15-16.
40. Underhill, *The Golden Sequence*, pp. 163-164.
41. Evelyn Underhill, *Man and the Supernatural* (New York: E. P. Dutton & Co., Inc., 1928), p. 199.
42. Underhill, *The Golden Sequence*, p. 179.
43. Underhill, *The Golden Sequence*, p. 180.
44. *The New Testament in Modern English*. Copyright, J. B. Phillips (New York: The Macmillan Co., 1958), pp. 332-333. Romans 8:26.
45. Underhill, *The Golden Sequence*, pp. 187-188.
46. Underhill, *The Golden Sequence*, p. 189.
47. Underhill, *Letters*, p. 300.
48. Underhill, *Light of Christ*, p. 84.
49. Underhill, *Light of Christ*, p. 87.
50. Underhill, *Fruits of the Spirit*, p. 16.
51. Underhill, *Immanence*, pp. 82-83.

SUGGESTED FURTHER READING[1]

Books in print may be ordered from the Cokesbury Book Store serving your territory. (Prices are subject to change.) Your local church, public, or college libraries may be able to lend "out-of-print" books to you. Note particularly the books marked with an asterisk (*). Also see books listed in "Notes," pp. 181-189.

FRANÇOIS FÉNELON

BOOKLETS

FÉNELON, FRANÇOIS. *Meditations for Every Day of the Month.* Cincinnati, Ohio: Forward Movement Publications, 412 Sycamore St. 15 cents.

FÉNELON, FRANÇOIS. *Reflections for Every Day of the Month* (Paternoster ser.). Springfield, Ill.: Templegate Publishers, Box 963. 35 cents.

BOOKS

FÉNELON, FRANÇOIS. *Letters to Men and Women.* Westminster, Md.: Newman Press, 1957. $4.00.

* FÉNELON, FRANÇOIS. *Letters and Reflections*, ed. by Thomas S. Kepler. Cleveland, Ohio: World Publishing Co., 1955. $1.75.

LITTLE, KATHARINE DAY. *François de Fénelon* (Study of a Personality). New York: Harper & Row, Inc., 1951. (Out-of-print.)

[1] **For further references and study, see books listed in NOTES, pp. 181-189.**

JOHN WESLEY

BOOKLETS

BRYAN, JOHN L. *John Wesley, the First Methodist.* Washington, D. C.: Board of Christian Social Concerns of The Methodist Church, 100 Maryland Ave. 75 cents.

* THOMAS, G. ERNEST. *Abundant Life Through Aldersgate.* Nashville: Methodist Evangelistic Materials, 1908 Grand Ave. 62 pages. 50 cents each; 12 or more, 40 cents each.

REED, BISHOP MARSHALL R. *Achieving Christian Perfection.* Nashville: Methodist Evangelistic Materials. 50 cents each; 12 or more copies for 40 cents each.

SELECMAN, CHARLES C. and GEORGE H. JONES. *The Methodist First Reader.* Nashville: Methodist Evangelistic Materials, 94 pages. 50 cents each; 12 or more, 40 cents each.

SIMS, LYDEL. *The Burning Thirst, A Story of John Wesley.* Nashville: Abingdon Press, © 1958. Small dimension paperback, 136 pages. (Out-of-print.)

Tell Me the Story of John Wesley (pictorial account). Nashville: Methodist Evangelistic Materials, 25 pages. 10 cents each; $8.00 for 100; 200 or more, 6 cents each.

Martin Luther's Preface to the Epistle to the Romans. Nashville: Methodist Evangelistic Materials. 15 cents each; 10 or more, 10 cents each.

BOOKS

BAKER, E. W. *A Herald of the Evangelical Revival* (A Critical Inquiry into the Relation of William Law and John Wesley and Beginnings of Methodism). Naperville, Ill.: Alec R. Allenson, n.d. $2.75.

BOWMER, JOHN C. *The Sacrament of the Lord's Supper in Early Methodism.* Nashville: Abingdon Press, n.d. $3.00.

BRAILSFORD, MABEL RICHMOND. *A Tale of Two Brothers, John and Charles Wesley.* New York: Oxford University Press, 1954. $4.50.

CANNON, WILLIAM R. *The Theology of John Wesley.* Nashville: Abingdon Press, n.d. $3.00.

CHURCH, LESLIE. *Knight of the Burning Heart.* New York: Abingdon Press, 1953. $1.75.

DESCHNER, JOHN. *John Wesley's Christology.* Dallas: Southern Methodist University Press, 1960. $4.50.

DOBREE, BONAMY. *Three Eighteenth Century Figures: Sara Churchill, John Wesley, and Giacomo Casanova.* London: Oxford University Press, 1962. $4.80.

DOUGHTY, WILLIAM L. *John Wesley, Preacher.* Naperville, Ill.: Alec R. Allenson, Inc., 1955. $3.50.

EDWARDS, MALDWYN LLOYD. *John Wesley and the Eighteenth Century.* Nashville: Abingdon Press, 1933. $2.50.

EDWARDS, MALDWYN LLOYD. *Sons to Samuel.* Nashville: Abingdon Press, n.d. $2.50.

FOSDICK, HARRY EMERSON, ed. *Great Voices of the Reformation.* New York: Modern Library, 1952 (G9). $2.95.

GREEN, JOHN BRAZIER. *John Wesley and William Law.* Naperville, Ill.: Alec R. Allenson, 1945. $3.00.

GREEN, JOHN R. *Short History of the English People.* Rev. ed., New York: E. P. Dutton & Co., 1952. Everyman ed., 2 vol., $1.95 each.

HADDAL, INGVAR. *John Wesley.* Translated from original Norwegian. Nashville: Abingdon Press, 1961. $3.50.

HARMON, BISHOP NOLAN B. *Understanding The Methodist Church.* Nashville: Abingdon Press, 1955. $1.00.

HIGGINS, PAUL L. *John Wesley: Spiritual Witness.* Minneapolis, Minn.: T. S. Denison & Co., 1960. $3.00.

HILL, A. WESLEY. *John Wesley Among the Physicians* (A Study of Eighteenth Century Medicine). Nashville: Abingdon Press, n.d. $2.00.

JEFFERY, THOMAS. *John Wesley's Religious Quest.* Fresco: Vantage Press, Inc., 1960. $5.00.

LEE, UMPHREY. *The Lord's Horseman.* Nashville: Abingdon Press, 1954. $2.75.

LEE, UMPHREY and WILLIAM WARREN SWEET. *A Short History of Methodism.* Nashville: Abingdon Press, 1956. $2.00.

LINDSTROM, HARALD. *Wesley and Sanctification.* Nashville: Abingdon Press, 1956. Paper, $2.25.

LUCCOCK, HALFORD E. and PAUL HUTCHINSON. *The Story of Methodism.* Nashville: Abingdon Press, n.d. $5.00.

MCCONNELL, FRANCIS J. *John Wesley.* Nashville: Abingdon Press, 1939. $4.50. Apex Books, paper, $1.75.

MCNEER, MAY and LYND WARD. *John Wesley.* Nashville: Abingdon Press, 1958. $2.50; paper, $1.25.

* SANGSTER, WILLIAM E. *The Path to Perfection* (An Examination and Restatement of John Wesley's Doctrine of Christian Perfection). Naperville, Ill.: Alec R. Allenson, Inc., 1960. $3.50.

SHERWIN, OSCAR. *John Wesley* (Friend of the People). New York: Twayne Publishers, 1961. $5.00.

SIMON, JOHN S. *John Wesley.* Nashville: Abingdon Press, 1921—1934. (5 vol. set). Vol. I, *John Wesley and the Religious Societies,* from 1703 to 1739; Vol. II, *John Wesley and the Methodist Societies,* from 1739 to 1746; Vol. III, *John Wesley and The Advance of Methodism,* from 1747 to 1757; Vol. IV, *John Wesley, The Master Builder,* from 1757 to 1772; Vol. V, *John Wesley, The Last Phase,* 1773 to 1791. $4.75 each.

STARKEY, L. M., JR. *The Work of the Holy Spirit* (A Study in Wesleyan Theology). Nashville: Abingdon Press, 1962. $3.00.

TELFORD, JOHN. *The Life of John Wesley*. Naperville, Ill.: Alec R. Allenson, Inc., 1953. $3.75.

THOMPSON, EDGAR W. *Wesley: Apostolic Man*. Naperville, Ill.: Alec R. Allenson, Inc., 1957. $2.25.

VULLIAMY, C. E. *John Wesley*. New York: Charles Scribner's Sons, 1932. Nashville: Abingdon Press, n.d. $4.00.

WARD, A. DUDLEY. *The Social Creed of The Methodist Church*. Nashville: Abingdon Press, 1961. $1.50.

WESLEY, JOHN. *Devotions and Prayers*, ed. by Donald E. Demaray. Grand Rapids, Mich.: Baker Book House, 1957. $1.50.

WESLEY, JOHN. *Explanatory Notes Upon the New Testament*. Naperville, Ill.: Alec R. Allenson, Inc., 1954. $3.75.

WESLEY, JOHN. *John Wesley's Prayers*, ed. by Frederick C. Gill. Nashville: Abingdon Press, 1952. $1.50.

WESLEY, JOHN. *Journal of John Wesley*, ed. by Hugh Martin. Naperville, Ill.: Alec R. Allenson, Inc., 1955. $2.50.

WESLEY, JOHN. *John Wesley's Journal*, as abridged by Nehemiah Curnock. New York: Philosophical Library, 1951. $3.75.

WESLEY, JOHN. *Journal of John Wesley*, ed. by Nehemiah Curnock. Nashville: Abingdon Press, n.d. (8 vol.) Available only in set. $35.00.

WESLEY, JOHN. *Letters of the Rev. John Wesley, A.M.*, ed. by John Telford. Nashville: Abingdon Press, n.d. (8 vol.) Available only in set. $35.00.

WESLEY, JOHN. *Selected Letters of John Wesley*, ed. by Frederick C. Gill. Nashville: Abingdon Press, © 1956. $3.50.

WESLEY, JOHN. *Selections from the Writings of John Wesley*, arr. by Herbert Welch. Nashville: Abingdon Press, n.d. $3.00.

WESLEY, JOHN. *Works of John Wesley*. Grand Rapids, Mich.: Zondervan Publishing House, 1958. 14 vol. $24.95.

WHITELEY, JOHN H. *Wesley's England*. (Allenson) Nashville: Abingdon Press, 1954. $3.25.

WILLIAMS, COLIN W. *John Wesley's Theology Today*. Nashville: Abingdon Press, 1960. $4.50.

EVELYN UNDERHILL

BOOKLET

UNDERHILL, EVELYN. *Selections*, arr. by Jean Parriss. Cincinnati 2, Ohio: Forward Movement Publications, 412 Sycamore St., 44 pages. 10 cents.

BOOKS

CROPPER, MARGARET. *Life of Evelyn Underhill*. Longmans, Green, Ltd., 6 Clifford St., London, W. 1., 1958. $7.00.

KEPLER, THOMAS S., comp. *The Evelyn Underhill Reader*. New York: Abingdon Press, 1962. $5.50.

UNDERHILL, EVELYN. *Concerning the Inner Life With the House of the Soul.* New York: E. P. Dutton & Co., 1947. $2.50.

UNDERHILL, EVELYN. *Fruits of the Spirit, Light of Christ, and Abba: Meditations Based on the Lord's Prayer.* New York: David McKay Co., 1956. $3.50.

UNDERHILL, EVELYN. *The Golden Sequence.* New York: Harper & Row, 1960. Torchbook. (out-of-print).

UNDERHILL, EVELYN. *The Letters of Evelyn Underhill*, ed. by Charles Williams. New York: David McKay Co., 1943. $4.25.

UNDERHILL, EVELYN. *The Mount of Purification.* New York: David McKay Co., © 1960. $3.50.

UNDERHILL, EVELYN. *Mysticism* (A Study in the Nature and Development of Man's Spiritual Consciousness). New York: E. P. Dutton & Co., 1912. $7.50; D73 paper, $1.95.

UNDERHILL, EVELYN. *Practical Mysticism.* New York: E. P. Dutton & Co., 1960. Everyman ed. D49 paper, $1.15.

UNDERHILL, EVELYN. *School of Charity, and Mystery of Sacrifice.* New York: David McKay Co., 1945. $3.50.

UNDERHILL, EVELYN. *Worship.* New York: Harper & Row, 1937. $4.00. Torchbook ,1957, $1.95.

PRONUNCIATION GUIDE

Abbe de Tourville .... Ah-BEH d'Tour-veele
antinomianism .... AN-teh-NOE-mih-an-izm
Assisi .... Ah-see-zee
Bishop Bossuet .... Boss-WAY
Bishop of Chalons .... Shall-ON
Bishop of Meaux .... Moe
Cahors .... Cah-ORE
Cambrai .... Cahm-BRAY
Collége du Plessis .... Co-LEZH d'Ples-SEE
De Noailles .... d'No-eye-ee
Dordogne River .... Door-DONE-yeh
Friedrich von Hügel .... Hoogel
Issy Conferences .... Ee-see
Madame de Maintenon .... Men-t'-NO
Madame Guyon .... Gee-OWN
Molinos .... Moe-lee-NOE
Pêrigord .... Pear-ee-GOAR
Saintonge .... San-TON-zh
Solesmes .... So-LAMB
solifidianism .... SOL-eh-FID-ih-ahn-ism
St. Cyr .... Sa-SEER
Versailles .... Ver-SAY

THE COVER

Each person's interpretation of the cover will be colored by his own experience and concern. The artist has combined in new ways some traditional Christian symbols: the *circle*—representing God, eternity, wholeness, perfection; *rays of light*—representing divine illumination, guidance, knowledge, direction; the modified *triquetra*—representing the triune God: Father, Son, and Holy Spirit; our three authors; and three classics. Note how the motif of the circle and its parts are used in the "C," "P," and "3."

The brushed tones of the *gray* and *sienna*, shading from dark to light, recall biblical references to darkness and light and symbolize stillness, thoughtfulness, and the illumination and growth of Christian understanding which come from God through study and prayer. *White* is the color of the Creator, purity, light, perfection; and *green,* the universal color of nature, signifies vitality, hope, and growth in the Christian life as one develops in Christian faith and action. *Gold* symbolizes the Glory of God, virtue, and value.

The artist, Mamie Harmon (the daughter of a Methodist minister, and a graduate of Wesleyan College, Macon, Georgia), who designed both the cover and the book's format, is well known here and abroad for her perceptive interpretations through various art forms. She is a writer as well as a designer and painter and has written on art subjects for the *Encyclopedia of World Art,* the *Dictionary of Folklore,* and other publications. She is also the designer of the Wesley Covenant prayer card, *I am no longer my own—but THINE.*

E463

LITERATURE HEADQUARTERS
Woman's Division of Christian Service
Board of Missions, The Methodist Church
7820 Reading Road, Cincinnati 37, Ohio
Price, $1.00